AF400774

EMPOWERED: ONE PLANET AT A TIME

STANDING UP FOR OUR PLANET AND OURSELVES

PATTY DREIER

FOREWORD BY ABERDEEN LEARY,
"WE CANNOT BE TOO LOUD"

Copyright © 2019 Patty Dreier

Pastel painting commissioned by Patty Dreier to illustrate *Empowered: One Planet at a Time* Copyright © 2019 Dan Sivek

All rights reserved.

Printed in the United States of America

Published by Author Academy Elite

P.O. Box 43, Powell, OH 43035

www.AuthorAcademyElite.com

All rights reserved. No part of this publication may be reproduced, stored in a retrieval system, or transmitted in any form or by any means—for example, electronic, photocopy, recording—without the prior written permission of the publisher. The only exception is brief quotations in printed reviews.

Paperback ISBN 978-1-64746-003-7

Hardcover ISBN 978-1-64746-004-4

Library of Congress Control Number: 2019917910

Cover design by Khurram Khan, www.khurramdesigns.com

Cover and book art by Dan Sivek, www.qartists.com

Photography of interior book art by Kathleen Dreier,

www.kathleendreier.com

WHAT READERS OF *EMPOWERED: ONE PLANET AT A TIME* ARE SAYING

You really painted a picture in my mind. I'm feeling inspired to make change.

This book gave me tools and resources to put my activism into action and gave me hope that I am capable of making the change that I desperately wish to see.

I truly enjoyed this book. It helped me trace the roots of who I am but more importantly why I am!

I feel much more empowered, confident, and ready to get started to try and make changes than I did before. I was one of those people who wanted to make a change but felt too intimidated to move forward. The exercises make it seem much less daunting!

It was a wonderful read.

While reading, you are our guide on our journey of growth, becoming empowered, and defining our core values: how cool is that?

An easy read for those at different levels of their journey, this book lays a sturdy foundation for readers to build on. For readers whose journeys have already begun, this book allows them to reaffirm their beliefs and add on to them from there.

Your exercises were a great way for readers to both look inside themselves and build a strong, knowledgeable plan. Each exercise seemed to be a very important step....

The fact that EMPOWERED is so personal and relatable makes the experience much more personal for the readers, too.

Sharing your stories as an elected official and how you listened to concerned citizens who came forward helps your audience see that standing for their beliefs and going to their elected officials isn't as scary as they thought.

Love the uniqueness of including your music!

This book had an impact on my own views regarding what I AM responsible for, and what I COULD BE responsible for, here on Earth.

It is really helpful for the reader to see your personal struggles with activism, and your advice is inspiring.

I think the rubrics were a really empowering element...

The story in Chapter 3 was powerful and inspiring. It helped me realize that while it can be hard to be an advocate for the Earth, there is power in developing relationships with others to build a stronger voice. I am hopeful that I am able to make a difference because I know I am not alone.

After reading the foreword…it's moving to hear someone in a similar age cohort have such strong opinions. In an ideal world, we wouldn't have environmental degeneration to deal with and in an ideal world we wouldn't have to wake up in the morning to solve uncomfortable and demanding problems, but I feel empowered, encouraged, and imbued with courage when someone so young shares such great ideals. Knowing that people who are on the 'path' think this way means to me that we, indeed, cannot be too loud.

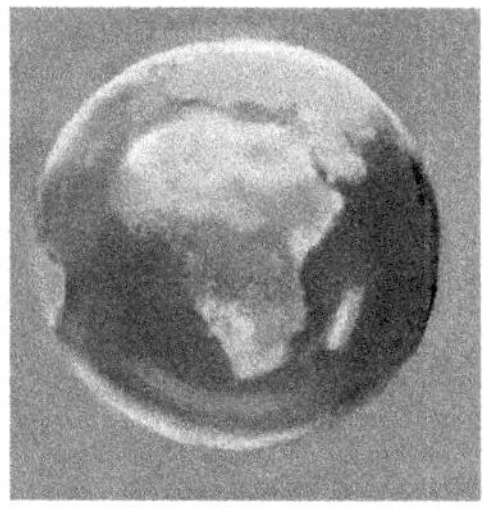

For young adults and their mentors

For a brighter future

CONTENTS

FOREWORD BY ABERDEEN LEARY

We Cannot Be Too Loud

When I was asked to write this foreword encouraging my peers to stand up for our environment, I was excited for the opportunity to put my emotions into words. I thought it would be an enjoyable, almost cathartic experience. Yet, as I began to outline my thoughts, I struggled to overcome intense feelings of anger and hopelessness. It infuriated me that here I was, a twenty-one year-old girl with a tiny apartment and thousands of dollars in college debt, giving my all to save the world, while no one around me seemed to be helping. I felt myself sliding further and further into a pessimistic resolve in which I decided it was impossible for our generation to heal the planet while so many factors were working against us. Then I thought, what choice do we have? If we continue on the same path we're on now, our legacy can be easily predicted.

If we don't stand up and begin making changes, we'll be remembered for our ignorance, an attitude heavily shaped by those who came before us. Our parents fell like dynamite on the planet, taking what they needed in an era of advancement with little consideration of the cost. We watched on as ecosystems were dismantled and species brought to extinction, not knowing our tiny styrofoam cup and plate were a part of the problem. We stared out the window as our parents filled the gas tank, unconscious of the link between what got us to school and what poisoned the ocean when an oil rig exploded halfway around the world. We saw our houses rise out of strong timber, knocking old-growth forests to the ground, and we stood by as that same timber went up in flames, alongside fossil fuels, to create the energy we used daily. We also embraced an unforeseen new enemy, plastic. Growing up in this era of oblivion meant our thirst was matched with bottled water, our hunger with snacks, each individually wrapped in their own packaging. We were handed our plastic plates with plastic spoons and plastic forks and were then asked how the world would digest a plastic island the size of Texas floating adrift in the Pacific. From day one our legacy has been destruction—but it doesn't have to stay that way.

Today, there are countless examples of people turning environmental challenges into opportunity. Proof of this can be seen as renewable energy becomes substantially more popular and advances in science and technology are put in place to reverse issues like ocean pollution and CO2 abundance. The decline of animal products and the poaching enterprise are also evident, with coal and other fossil fuels trailing them as they slowly lose popularity. In total, this means people are beginning to care. We're beginning to catch the attention of not only individuals and their families, but large corporations and government officials, too. Our vote matters, our dollar counts, and we've proven our voices can make waves of change.

As Generation Y and Z, we stand at a unique place. We are the next politicians, the next scientists, and the next teachers. Soon, we will be the leaders with enough power to shape the patterns and practices of those around us—and our message must be clear. Change needs to happen. Still, it must be recognized that no person or country can make this change alone. This crisis crosses oceans, continents, and political borders and can only be mended with all of us, together, fighting for our planet.

We know the future we envision is unsteady and we know we have the ability to transform it. It will take courage and it will take confidence, but we have both in us. We must mobilize and empower each other to stand up for our planet. This is our moment.

Find your platform. Be unwavering in your demands. We are just as much citizens of this Earth as any businessman or politician standing in our way and we have the right to call for a healthy planet for ourselves, and for the future. So, let our voices rise. Let them be heard from ocean to ocean–in the cities, in the villages, in the parliament. They cannot be—*we* cannot be—too loud.

1

STANDING UP FOR YOUR FUTURE BEGINS WITH YOU

Your Earth, Your Present, Your Future

Great, I hope I don't kill the Father of Earth Day. These were my first thoughts after I accepted the responsibility of being U.S. Senator Gaylord Nelson's chauffeur for the day. The year was 1988. I was a graduate student at the University of Wisconsin-Stevens Point College of Natural Resources. These were the kinds of tasks delegated to students from time to time—and I guess you'd call me "the lucky one" this time though my good fortune didn't come without risks and fears. Of course, I trusted my own driving ability. But, what about the people who would share the road with me that day when I was driving this famous man—someone who had changed my state, my country and the world? The other drivers wouldn't know I was carrying such precious cargo.

When I accepted responsibility for driving Senator Nelson, it meant I had to check out a state car from the motor pool, drive

1

to Oshkosh about an hour away to pick him up, then drive him back to Stevens Point for some special events including the opening of a new nature trail on campus. It would be an unforgettable experience to walk the Trail of Reflections with him and watch his reaction when he came upon his own famous words carved by students into a sign beside the trail there. But first, I had to get him safely to Stevens Point.

Not only was Senator Nelson the man who conceptualized what developed into the first Earth Day when he was in the U.S. Senate in 1970, but he had been Wisconsin's Governor and a Wisconsin Senator before that.[1] Nearly his whole life had been devoted to public service. He was known most for his leadership on environmental issues and for his efforts to preserve natural areas for future generations. Why, even Vince Lombardi of Green Bay Packer fame had once called Senator Nelson the "nation's #1 conservationist"[2] during one of Nelson's re-election campaigns.

On that first Earth Day, April 22, 1970, an estimated 20 million Americans rose up in environmental protests, clean ups, and "teach-ins" across our nation.[3] I was only nine years old then. I learned later how this mass movement of people had shifted the political agenda of the United States.

Elected leaders in Washington, D.C. heard the message loud and clear and got busy enacting environmental laws that would give us cleaner water, cleaner air and would protect endangered species. In fact, the first Earth Day created a wave of change with twenty-eight pieces of significant environmental legislation enacted in the decade that followed.[5,6] Year after year, the annual Earth Day event would also spark environmental discussions, service projects, special

> BECAUSE THE LOCAL ORGANIZING EFFORT WAS EMPOWERING, THE INVOLVEMENT OF SO MANY ORGANIZERS ALSO HELPED TO ENSURE THAT EARTH DAY LEFT A LASTING LEGACY.
> –ADAM ROME[4]

events, and educational programs as people across the world joined the movement. Not only would I be the driver for a man who changed the world, but I would have a once-in-a-lifetime opportunity to meet a personal hero of mine.

When the day came, I was nervous to say the least. Not only did I have my concerns for safety on the road, but I also wondered, *what would I say to this important man?* Even as a graduate student studying natural resources and environmental education, I admit I felt insignificant. His world had to have been so much different from my own! Why, in his former government roles, he had represented *millions* of people; I was only one.

When I picked up Senator Nelson in Oshkosh, he was wearing a long black coat and carrying a black briefcase. He sat in the back seat behind the front passenger seat which gave me a chance to sneak a look at him every now and then in the rearview mirror. He pulled out some papers and looked like he was concentrating on something—maybe a speech he would make in Stevens Point? While I didn't want to disturb him, I sure was not about to let this whole one-hour journey go by without saying anything to this man. So, I took a deep breath and said, "Thank you for founding Earth Day." Senator Nelson met my eyes in the rearview mirror. Then he responded to my expression of gratitude by passing the thanks on to other people. I paraphrase: *The credit goes to the people who stood up and spoke up in their own places and in their own ways to make sure changes would happen about issues that mattered to them.*

A WORLD OF POSSIBILITIES

I don't recall any more talk for the rest of the trip as Senator Nelson went back to working on his papers. I used the time to think about what he had shared—that it was those who voiced their concerns who deserved the credit for changing the world since Earth Day 1970. Little did I know then, I would go on to co-found the first German-American Earth Day in 1991 with my German colleagues in Würzburg. German-American Earth Day would connect German children and American military school children with their teachers and community leaders each year for fifteen years (as long as the U.S. military had a presence there). It would build international friendships and a common understanding about the planet they shared. Little did I know then I would run a campaign of my own in 2010 and represent 71,000 people for eight years in public office. As Portage County Executive, I would work with citizens who wanted to stand up and speak up in their own places and ways to make sure changes would happen on issues that mattered to them—like water issues—in central Wisconsin and the whole State of Wisconsin.

On that day in 1988, Senator Nelson arrived safely in Stevens Point thanks to his careful driver and the stars aligning to make sure it was so. Over the past thirty years, I have often thought about those few words we shared in the car and how the Father of Earth Day's words represent a world of possibilities for a brighter future. The true power for change in 1970 came from the people. And it still comes from the people who stand up and speak up today.

A FUTURE DESIGNED BY YOU

This book was written to give you the tools needed to be a true power for change in your own community and in the larger world. I wrote it with an intention of helping you develop into your strongest, most empowered self so you can stand up and speak up with confidence today and play an active role in designing your own future on this planet.

In the pages to come, I share some lessons I have learned the easy way and some I have learned the hard way along my journey of becoming empowered. You will find practical exercises, methods, and action steps intermingled with stories to offer real world examples. Most of the stories come from my life as I have lived in many places in the United States, but also in Europe for nearly six years. Though this book has been shaped through an American lens, my sincerest hope is that the timeless concepts and methods will offer value for every reader no matter where you live in the world.

As you read this book, there are times when I challenge you to pause and take a self-assessment or complete a personal exercise. The checklists and workbook exercises are intended to offer practical ways to immerse yourself in this book's content, but also to help you discover more about yourself. These self-discoveries will help build a stronger foundation that prepares you for standing up with more confidence for what you believe in. Some checklists are also offered as tools you can use later when you take action on issues that matter to you.

This book will make a difference in your life as it helps you discover the powerhouse you are at your very core. As you develop your know-how to become an active player in creating the kind of local and global world you need and desire today and for your future, you will never be the same again. Neither will the rest of the world when you turn your know-how into action—and that is exactly what is needed! Now more than ever, we need to transform our communities and the ways we live on our planet to address critical challenges and find a better balance. It will take great social and environmental movements of concerned citizens who get involved as agents for change. Those movements will need inspiring leaders and team members—like you. When you become empowered and develop your skills for taking action on issues that matter, it forever serves you and the causes you believe in. Life becomes even more satisfying because you know you are making a purposeful, positive difference.

Empowered people don't let the world pass them by. They get involved because they know they have something to contribute. They know their perspective matters and their voice counts. They want to play an active role rather than settle for what others may have in mind. How about you? Are you interested in designing your future? Is there a cause or opportunity calling your name? Are there challenges you need to overcome? Do you have something great to offer us all? *I think you do, so let's get started!*

WHAT MATTERS TO YOU?

Glance at the news headlines on any given day, and you will probably see there are some things that seem to be going well and some things that do not seem to be going well in your community, your country, and our world. Certainly, one newscast or one headline doesn't tell a whole story (or even the truth sometimes), but they can give you a general sense of some issues and opportunities around you. When you dig deeper and check multiple information sources to verify the facts, then step back for a wider view and different perspectives on the issue, you will begin to clarify your position on the matter. Consider asking yourself these five questions as you figure out where you stand on an issue:

1. **What do I know about the issue?**

2. **How do I feel about the issue?**

3. **Is it going the way I would like it to go?**

4. **Do I have some knowledge, skills, ideas or other resources to offer?**

5. **How does my/our future relate to this issue?**

Then you will be faced with an important choice: Will you be a bystander and let others make decisions <u>for</u> you on the issue or opportunity, or will you stand up and speak up for yourself?

All too often, we leave it up to others. That might come after we make an excuse such as "I am too busy." Sometimes, we become overwhelmed by the size of the issue or the number of issues needing attention or how far away "ground zero" may be on the matter. We might not feel we have the right set of skills or know the right people to make a difference. And sometimes, we might even feel afraid. I have done or experienced all of these at one time or another—leaving it up to others, thinking I was too busy, being overwhelmed, feeling inadequate, believing I lacked connection with the necessary people, AND feeling afraid.

Just like focusing a camera lens helps you create a clearer image of the subject matter in a close-up photo, focusing your sights on a single issue or opportunity can help you frame a more distinct picture of your subject of interest or concern. What issue is most concerning to you? What opportunity most interests you? Select one, then narrow the focus or scope so you can zero in on the details. When you narrow the focus, it makes your efforts more manageable and increases your chances of making a difference. It also helps you overcome a sense of being overwhelmed or feeling inadequate. A narrower scope supports you in gathering the right information and knowing who the main players may be. It allows you to become laser focused on your desired goal. One barrier after another is more easily overcome when you focus on a single goal. Focusing on the change you most desire clears the way for you to move ahead.

WHERE DO YOU STAND?

Let's use an example from my experience to illustrate how answering the above questions helped me develop my stand on a top issue of concern. This example comes from my time as elected County Executive of Portage County, Wisconsin—a position of leadership in county government. Citizens in our county came forward with concerns about water quality and I shared their concerns. Let's answer the five questions:

1. **What do I know about the issue?**

   - *Except if they are buying water from an outside source because their own water is contaminated, all citizens in Portage County depend on groundwater for their drinking water source.*

   - *In nature, water usually contains less than 1 milligram of nitrate-nitrogen per liter (one part per million). Significantly higher levels often indicate water contaminated by human practices. Nitrate contamination in groundwater originates primarily from agricultural pesticides, manure spreading, and septic or sewage treatment sources.[7, 8] Higher concentrations of nitrates in drinking water can harm or kill unborn babies, infants, and children when it prevents proper oxygen flow in the child's bloodstream. Higher concentrations of nitrates are also suspected of causing other health problems and cancers.[9]*

   - *Some concerned citizens in Portage County have come forward with nitrate test results for their private wells which are over the safe drinking water standard of 10 parts per million (ppm). One citizen had an alarming 68 ppm after multiple tests confirmed this result.*

   - *Nitrates are like the "canary in the gold mine" for water. When there are water quality problems with nitrates, there are likely other contaminants in the water, too.[10] Nitrates are easier and cheaper to test for than many other contaminants. This explains why nitrate testing is commonly used on a first round of water tests.*

   - *Not only is this a health issue, but it is also an economic one. It costs municipalities with public water systems thousands of dollars to bring contaminated groundwater into compliance with safe drinking water standards and these costs are passed on to citizens through water rates on utility bills. A village in our county had to drill several wells to find water within nitrate ranges which could be treated to reach safe drinking water standards for their residents. The city took a public well station offline because groundwater pumped from that area was more highly contaminated with nitrates. Unsafe water can negatively affect property values and sales.*

- *Some citizens with private wells have tried drilling new wells to find better groundwater. Even after making this significant financial investment, they didn't yet find groundwater safe to drink.*

- *Some citizens bear the cost of expensive nitrate removal systems installed in their homes. Sometimes nitrates are so high in the water a home treatment system can't fix the problem to make the water safe to drink; they must buy water for their home use.*

2. How do I feel about the issue?

- *I feel strongly people should have safe drinking water available to them when they turn on the faucet and should not have to buy water because their own water is polluted.*

- *Our county needs to protect public health and our children—born and unborn. People need safe water to drink in order to be healthy.*

- *Water pollution costs everyone—those who have water provided by a public utility and those who have private wells.*

- *It is unacceptable for our county to go forward without helping our citizens know if their water is safe or not safe to drink—especially when many people cannot afford to pay for water tests or don't know to have it tested.*

- *Our county needs to be a leader in helping our citizens have a better future with cleaner water which starts with educating our whole community so we can work together to protect our water resources.*

3. **Is it going the way I would like it to go?**

- *No. Some citizens have come forward to say their water was tested by a certified laboratory and determined to be unsafe to drink. They are rightfully concerned. To date, not enough is being done about it.*

- *We don't know how many citizens are unknowingly drinking unsafe water. We don't know how extensive the problem is though we suspect it is widespread because contaminants can readily flow through the sandy, porous soils found across much of our county.*

- *We aren't sure about the major causes though we have some hypotheses. We need proof so we can work on solutions with those directly involved.*

4. **Do I have some knowledge, skills, ideas or other resources to offer?**

- *Yes. I know some water experts connected with our local university who also manage a water testing laboratory. They know of other Wisconsin counties which conducted countywide water quality studies. Because there is sampling done in plots across the whole county, every home won't need an individual water test. We will be able to gather a "big picture" of our water quality situation. Together, we will develop a strategy for something similar which will also be tied to the soil types and uses of the land (forested, agriculture, etc.). University students will gather the water samples with landowner permission under the guidance of university faculty and in coordination with the county.*

- *The cost of the study is $25,000. As County Executive, my job is to develop the county budget, so I will add $25,000 to our budget next year when the countywide study will be conducted for its first time. In addition, I will propose $5,000 be set aside every year in a special account to save up money to replicate the countywide water quality study in the future so we can track progress and changes. After five years, we will have accrued $25,000. This regular budget practice will ensure we have funding for the next countywide study when we want to repeat it.*

- *After the study is completed, we will hold public information sessions to inform citizens and conduct other outreach to target groups that should know about the results. We will discuss how we can protect our water resources together.*

5. How does my/our future relate to this issue?

- *The vibrancy of Portage County's future depends on providing its citizens with safe drinking water everywhere—at their homes, in businesses, in towns, in villages, and in our city.*

- *A baseline study which gathers and maps data across our county and correlates it with soil types and land uses will give us a broader picture of where our trouble spots are found and what may be causing them. Then, we will be able to focus our education and outreach in those target areas and with those target populations.*

Do you see how these five questions helped me develop my stance on the water quality issue in our county? They also helped me develop some logical action steps and recommendations for moving forward on the issue.

Did I have any fears in dealing with the water quality study? Yes! I remember fearing what we would find. Yet, I knew we needed to know so we could focus our efforts on protecting the health of our citizens and finding solutions. I also remember being afraid individuals, businesses, and industries might be angry—especially large contributors to our water quality problem.

If I had let my fears hold me back, I would not have been doing the right thing for today or tomorrow. Had it not been for the citizens who came forward with concerns about their water quality at home, I may not have become aware of the issue. Without hearing from citizens in a village about how they had to try several times to drill a well and find water with nitrate levels low enough to treat for compliance with safe drinking water standards, I may not have learned how widespread and expensive the water quality issue was in our county. And that is the beauty of communities! There are so many different perspectives to be understood to get the whole picture on any issue or opportunity.

When it comes to human communities, people make the place. Sharing our values, choosing our livelihoods and lifestyles, volunteering, and reaching out to care for our neighbors are a few ways we shape our neighborhoods and communities. When it came to Portage County and our water quality issue, I knew it was right to want a safe and healthy place to live and raise families. That took precedence over everything else. It outweighed every challenge or obstacle. Protecting the quality of life and the health of our citizenry became an investment in protecting the quality of our future. The baseline study gave us critical data to serve as a starting point against which we could measure our progress (or lack thereof) when we replicated the study in the future.

STANDING UP FOR ENVIRONMENT AND COMMUNITY = STANDING UP FOR YOU

As the water quality example points out very well: *Our quality of life is directly related to the quality of our environment.*[11] Separating the two is impossible anywhere. If our environment is sick, how can we be healthy and live well? If we drink contaminated water every day, how can we live a healthy life? When someone says, "It's not my problem," they are essentially saying their own quality of life is not their problem.

In a nutshell, that is why this book has been written. Too many people are disengaged from actively participating in solving local and global issues that directly affect them. Without their involvement, they miss out and we all miss out on their voices and energies. This book is intended to prepare and empower readers like you to address social and environmental issues with courage and confidence because now more than ever, there are serious matters that need attention and buy-in across masses of people. Knowing why you want to stand up on issues, knowing how to bring about changes, and believing in yourself and your capabilities are cornerstones of being empowered. When you are empowered and stand up for your environment and your community it means you understand you have something to contribute and something to gain. In our communities, social problems such as hunger, poverty, drug addiction, crime, and blighted neighborhoods (to name a few) are interconnected with environmental issues. On our planet, environmental

> TAKING RESPONSIBILITY FOR PLANET EARTH—YOUR MACRO ENVIRONMENT—IS THE SAME THING AS TAKING RESPONSIBILITY FOR YOUR OWN FUTURE.

problems such as air pollution, tropical deforestation, and plastics in the oceans (to name a few) are related to social issues like transportation, economics, and consumer choices or behaviors. Taking responsibility for Planet Earth—your macro environment—is the same thing as taking responsibility for your own future.

IT'S YOUR BUSINESS

Just in case you don't think it is your business to stand up on issues beyond your community's borders or your country's borders, consider this:

- The rate of species extinction is accelerating. We humans are the cause. One million species are threatened with disappearing from Earth forever in the next few decades unless we do something.[12] Some scientists estimate three species are lost every minute and up to 150 species become extinct daily on our planet.[13] Natural populations of animals, plants and other living things simply cannot adapt as fast as humans are destroying or degrading their habitats and changing the planet. Extinction is your business because this is your web of life on Earth. Your lifeblood is being compromised.

- Every day the population of people on Earth increases by over 220,000.[14, 15] This is your business because each of them will share the planet's finite resources with you.

- Every day, more carbon dioxide and methane gases are added to Earth's atmosphere—much of it by human activities.[16] This is trapping heat and warming up our planet. The accelerated rate of warming is causing our polar ice caps to melt which, in turn, is causing sea levels to rise. This is one of many catastrophic effects and chain reactions caused by adding carbon dioxide and methane gases to Earth's atmosphere. Global warming is your business because it affects human and natural communities everywhere and in significant ways.

These issues present just a few reasons why it is important to think about the whole planet as "your business." Certainly, there is a lot more to each one of the above issues and I hope you will investigate them further. The bottom line is that there has never been a greater need for each of us to be informed and active citizens of the Earth. The extraordinary level of interconnectedness today across our planet which is less than 8,000 miles in diameter means environmental, economic, political, social, cultural and ethical issues anywhere in the world affect us all. When we think only about our own life, our own interests, and our own bottom line, we only see a small part of the picture. When we think only about our own community or our own country, we may overlook vital connections. Keeping the whole Earth in mind is your business because this whole planet is your global community, environment, and home.

Maybe you are asking: *How can I make a difference as just one person in the sea of so many in my community, region or state, not to mention across a whole planet?* While the first Earth Day was just one day, it changed the world. On April 22, 1970, individuals—some of them like you—also wondered if they could make a difference and they stood up anyway. They knew their environment was their business. They made their voices heard. They didn't shrink from the challenges, they made strong stands for a better future. By getting involved in their own meaningful ways in their local communities, they turned the tide. They created an extraordinary movement that made an impact beyond what many of them had ever dreamed possible. It started with one person—U.S. Senator Gaylord Nelson. But, without other people standing up and insisting they be heard by their elected officials, it would have been just a senator's pipedream.

The same applies today but with more urgency due to the way humans have pushed the limits on Earth. In order to deal with today's complex local and global issues, it will take a sea of individuals—people who are ready, willing, and able to stand up and stand strong in their unique ways to see the necessary changes through. If you do not already see yourself as capable of being one of these much-needed agents for change, this book will equip you for the role. If you are already a change maker, my goal is for this book to bolster your efforts.

Tackling a local issue starts locally—in your home, neighborhood, school or university, and community. Tackling a global issue also starts where you are. That's one of the many blessings of having everything interconnected on our planet. Don't worry that the issue seems daunting or the world seems too big or your community seems too small. Local and global solutions always start in the same place—with you and your voice. Whether you want to see changes happen or prevent unfavorable changes from happening, it all comes down to you and your voice.

When things are going well, they may not stay that way unless we do something about making sure they do. It might mean thanking somebody. It might mean sharing our point of view about how helpful or positive something is. Let's not forget: *When you decide to be silent on an issue, it is the same as taking a stand on that issue.* It is your choice, but when you are silent for whatever

WHEN YOU ARE SILENT ON AN ISSUE, IT IS THE SAME AS TAKING A STAND ON IT.

the reason, you give your power to others. You defer to them and let them make decisions for you.

When you are eligible to vote and do not register and show up to vote, this is another way to give your power away to others. When you do not reach out to your elected officials or to other leaders (whether you are of voting age or not), you are allowing them to make choices *for* you. I am glad to say that hundreds of times while I was in public office, I received feedback from people (youth and adults) who wanted to share their input and experiences about issues, ask for help, express their concerns, share their visions, or just say thanks. Without their communication with me or my outreach to them to ask for feedback, how could I know what was on their minds or if I was on the right track? Even when I chose a different track than a citizen had preferred, their input gave me a better understanding of different points of view and valuable food for thought to use along the way as a community leader.

I remember walking behind Gaylord Nelson on the Trail of Reflections at Schmeeckle Reserve in Stevens Point, Wisconsin, that day in 1988 as he paused to read his quote carved on the wooden trail sign there. His quote was: "The idea that we can't afford to protect the environment…is wrong. If we continue to allow degradation of the country's resources, the ultimate balancing is going to be between society and nature—and we'll be bankrupt." Gaylord Nelson's sign is still there.[17] More importantly, his example is too.

Your future is quite literally *in your hands*. It is up to you to decide how you will handle that immense responsibility. The choices are totally up to you. Whether you stand up as one empowered individual or you join with a few others or you join with 20 million others, I am sure you will amaze yourself and you will never be the same. It all starts with the nature of who you are and how you develop and tap your inner sources of strength. *Turn the page, and let's dive deeply into those depths!*

2

THE NATURE OF POWER WITHIN YOU

Your Roots, Your Experiences

What do you care about so deeply you are willing to stand up for it? How will you know you are ready? The answers to these questions lie at the heart of who you are. The better you know yourself from your roots to the person you are today, the clearer you will understand the nature of power within you and what matters most to you—two fundamental understandings for being successful as an agent for change.

You probably have more power than you think. You are also stronger than you may know. Throughout our lives, most of us continue to grow in our understanding about the nature of the power within us. With every test of our mettle, we learn more about ourselves—our core values, our strengths and weaknesses, and our hopes. The more life experiences we have and reflect upon, the greater our ability to build our courage and confidence.

ASSESS YOUR COURAGE AND CONFIDENCE

Let's do a quick assessment. How would you rate your courage and confidence? Using the scale provided, rate yourself by answering the following eight statements on the *Courage and Confidence Self-Assessment* below. Save your answers. You will need them later.

	1 Strongly Disagree	2 Disagree	3 Neutral	4 Agree	5 Strongly Agree
I know what I stand for.					
I have courage.					
I know where my courage comes from.					
I am confident I know my strengths.					
I am confident I know my weaknesses.					

I know how to restore my confidence when it is shaken.					
I am capable of being an agent for change.					
I am empowered to take on any challenge I set my mind to accepting.					

Instead of settling for what life brings our way, confident and courageous people—people who believe in themselves—go out and choose the future they want for themselves and work to make it happen. Isn't this the kind of life we desire? One of our own choosing with dreams of our own making?

BUILD ON YOUR FOUNDATIONS

Through the exercises in this chapter, you will probably begin to see yourself in a new light. The activities will help you clarify your core values—foundations in your life—and the reasons why those values are important to you. Building on your values, you will be able to develop your most convincing positions on issues and stand strong. When you challenge yourself or encounter a situation that puts you to the test (like it or not), you find out what you are made of. In that discovery, the nature of power within you shines through.

Let me share a story to illustrate what I mean. This is a story about a difficult situation which reinforced my values:

I awoke at about 2 a.m. with someone pounding on my dorm room door in the residence hall where I was living on campus. This person was yelling over and over again: "sunshine, sunshine, sunshine" as she pounded repeatedly on my door. I got out of bed and opened my door. There stood Ellen, wide-eyed with fists frozen in mid-air. She stopped mid-word, "sun-." I could see she was inebriated. As I looked around, there were four or five other women standing there including our RA (Residence Hall Advisor) who was our "go-to" if we needed anything on our dorm wing during that semester. Everyone became quiet. I don't think they expected me to be "home" in my dorm room that night.

Let me stop the story there. What would you have done if this had happened to you? There are any number of ways to respond, but what would you have done and why?

Now, let me share the rest of the story:

I walked past Ellen, looked into the eyes of the RA who had been letting it happen, and went down the hall without saying a word. And then it occurred to me: I had been hearing the word, "sunshine" frequently as I passed some of them in the hallway over the past few weeks. Ellen and her friends knew I had declined to do drugs with them. They knew I was aware that some of them were drug dealers since I walked into my shared dorm room last semester to find my roommate with them sorting marijuana into smaller plastic bags. This semester, I had gotten a room transfer and paid for a single room. Now I understood something else: They had a secret nickname for me—at least it was secret until this night when I realized

Ellen had been yelling, "Sunshine, Sunshine, Sunshine" with a capital *S*.

By the time I returned to my room a few minutes later, the group in the hallway had dispersed. All was quiet. The next day, I talked with my RA about it. She felt badly about allowing it to happen. If I let it, this event could become a distraction and interfere with my university education. I had been working so hard to build my future. Being harassed about not doing drugs could undermine my focus on achieving this semester's goals. Right then, I made decisions for myself: *I would move on. I would carry my head high. I would maintain a strong focus on my educational goals in alignment with my roots and values.* And my courage grew.

Was it difficult? *Yes.* Was it sometimes uncomfortable? *Absolutely.* But they had made their choices and I had made mine. Our paths had connected on the wing of a dormitory, but diverged when it came to the very different ways we chose to experience our lives. I never heard the nickname, "Sunshine," spoken in my presence again.

Today, what happened to me would be called "bullying." No matter what name is given to this kind of experience or who it happens to (ourselves or others), it requires us to stand up in our own way and rise above it. Each one of us is worthy of so much more in our relationships and in our communities. Looking back, I realize I received an unexpected gift that night when the experience strengthened my resolve as it did. No longer was I unsure about the significance of my goals in life. In fact, it gave me an unwavering belief in myself and the "sunny" idea that I could bring value to make the world a better place.

Almost forty years have passed since I was awakened from more than a night's sleep. Not only did this experience bolster my resolve, it made me more acutely aware of the hard knocks in life—knocks that happen to all of us from time to time.

> NOTHING IN LIFE IS TO BE FEARED, IT IS ONLY TO BE UNDERSTOOD. NOW IS THE TIME TO UNDERSTAND MORE, SO THAT WE MAY FEAR LESS.
> –MARIE CURIE[18]

They may come from other people and circumstances around us. They may come because of certain paths or preferences we have chosen for ourselves. We may have been born with them or have had them passed down to us through our family or heritage. No matter when or how the hard knocks have come, we have choices. We can let them keep us down and distract us, or we can put them behind us. We gain extra strength when we rise above and use them to remind us what we stand for and why.

REFLECT ON YOUR OWN STORY

Reflecting on our own life story can help us identify hard knocks but also the doors that have opened in our life to give us unique opportunities and perspectives. Reflecting on our own story gives us glimpses at where our fullest potential may lie. When we identify our most impactful experiences (good or bad), they help us clarify our values. This gives us a sense of where our strongest stances on issues may be able to take hold and grow. Like reflecting on my Sunshine story has done for me, these reflections about difficult experiences in our lives also give us a chance to leave the hard knocks behind. We can choose to turn them into sources of compelling drive and purpose. We can use them to enhance our capacities for standing up and persisting to make necessary changes in our world. *We can let them empower us.*

If you are not sure of social or environmental issues where you may be most impactful, the exercise below will help you explore the possibilities and discover your leading platforms for making change happen. As you trace the roots of your life to identify your most impactful experiences, they will highlight areas where you may be able to make a significant difference. As you become more sure of yourself and your core values, you will enhance the nature of power within yourself. Let me show you what I mean.

DISCOVER PLATFORMS AND PIVOT POINTS OF COURAGE BY TRACING YOUR ROOTS

I've laid out a simple outline of questions below. Briefly answering the questions can help you gain perspective on your own values and platforms for action (those issues you might take a stand on). The questions can also help you identify what I will call, *pivot points of courage*—those central experiences which give you foundations of uncommon strength and power that can guide you in any number of directions.

Setting/Community: Where did you grow up? What was it like? What stands out about your home, neighborhood and/or community?

Family: What stands out about the relationships you had growing up? Who were the main players? What traditions stand out? Who influenced you most and why?

Activities: What did you enjoy doing? Where did you spend your time?

Friends/Mentors: Who were the main players and what did they teach you? What stands out about relationships with people beyond family relationships in your life?

School: What stands out about subjects, teachers, school, and education within and beyond four walls?

Environment: What stands out about your environment and community?

Significant Events: What significant events and/or conditions shaped you?

Let me use my own story as an example. Since experiences of childhood and youth significantly shape us, I will consider some aspects of my upbringing. Mostly, though, I will focus on my pre-teen, teen, and early twenties in answering the questions. You can choose whatever time window makes the most sense for you to get at the core of why you are the way you are today.

Setting/Community: *I grew up in a small city in Wisconsin where our family lived in an historic octagon house built in the 1850's. It had cool features like secret hiding places and hidden pathways. It became a museum after we lived in it. We later moved to a neighborhood of seven houses in a wide countryside ten miles from town. There was a long bus ride to and from school each day. We grew a large vegetable garden in our backyard.*

Family: *Our family was blended. I have two half-sisters and one full sister and a little brother who died shortly after he was born. We always had a family dog. My dad was a down to earth guy. He went to school only up through the eighth grade, but he was one of the smartest people I have ever known. Dad worked in a factory. He was the primary gardener of the family. He also fished and hunted so our family often had wild fish and game to go with our home-grown garden vegetables. Mom was a high school graduate. She worked in our local school district. She had natural talent as an artist and musician and supported me in developing my own art and music talents. My siblings and I grew up helping Mom who had debilitating rheumatoid arthritis and countless surgeries. As her disease progressed, I learned a lot about medical systems and community aids for people with disabilities.*

Activities: *Our family camped. We traveled on weekends to various campgrounds and places where we would explore, hike and swim. Sometimes there were exciting encounters with wildlife. Later we had a cabin in woods so vast we could get lost in them—and we did. We had frequent family gatherings with grandparents, cousins, aunts, and uncles. I loved to sing and taught myself to play guitar. I composed and performed my music. As a teen, I had a job in the Youth Conservation Corps which involved a six-week program near Lake Superior in northern Wisconsin. We did hands-on conservation projects. I enjoyed bicycling, hiking, and learning about the plants and animals around our neighborhood. I was good at and enjoyed art of any kind and writing, including poetry.*

Friends/Mentors: *I had a few teachers who stood out as mentors—one in science, one in English, and one in music. My closest friend was (and still is) someone who loved art, music and the outdoors.*

School: *I was accepted to the music program at a university in Wisconsin where I studied vocal music. I originally intended to be a music teacher. After a year, I switched my major to another love: science. I went on to earn a bachelor's and a master's degree in science. The field of environmental education became my passion when I discovered it was multi-disciplinary which meant it could integrate all subjects including art, music and science. The most memorable experiences related to my schooling were always outdoor activities and field trips when I got to explore new places.*

Environment: *There was a creek down the road from our home. I walked or bicycled to it frequently and was fascinated with watching it change over time. My dad taught me a lot about nature—trees, birds, and gardening. It became my lifelong passion to learn more. Integrating the arts, language, and nature were my favorite ways to learn about and appreciate my natural environment. For example, I wrote a song on my guitar for tree-planting ceremonies, I painted birds, and I read writings of* *famous naturalist writers such as John Burroughs, Henry David Thoreau, and John Muir.*

Significant Events: *I saw both my mom and my dad stand up for what they believed in. Dad did it at work. Mom did it in our community and for our family when there was an incident involving someone in our neighborhood who attacked my sister. Our family lived modestly, but there was a time of tremendous financial challenge when I was in high school. I learned to be resourceful and entrepreneurial. For example, I remember finding and selling antique bottles found in an old dump down the road. I also sold my artwork. In my early twenties, I married my college sweetheart. My husband joined the U.S. Army with his specialty related to environmental and public health. His duty assignments gave us a chance to live in many different places and environments. From metropolitan areas like San Antonio, Texas, to remote places like North Pole, Alaska. From the prairies of Nebraska to the Pacific Northwest and Washington State. We also lived in Germany for six years and traveled widely to explore different places and cultures.*

Let's stop there. Can you take a guess at my values and the platforms for action in my life? Given the snapshot of part of my life above, is it any wonder I developed enthusiasm for nature and the arts? Can you guess how I might have developed my spirit for seeing the world as one community? Is it any wonder in my later years as an elected official I co-led a march on our state's capitol related to the rights of people with disabilities? The first community action I took was when I wrote a letter to the editor thanking the woman who bought the octagon house to turn it into a museum. Can you see where my courage and interest in that platform arose? How about my advocacy on water conservation mentioned in the previous chapter?

Because I have such deep love for this planet in my roots and in my heart, I stand up fearlessly for it. That's where this book came from—a dream to influence more people across the world in hopes they will stand up for the Earth with passion in their hearts, too.

Considering the template and my example above, what platforms have begun to take shape in your own life? Dig deep. Standing up for yourself and your planet requires you to know *why* at the heart of things. Moving toward a better future starts with who you already are and what you already know. When it comes from your heart and your personal experiences, you will have a stronger stance because you will be more passionate and convincing. When you own it deep inside, you will discover the power within you and pivot points for your own fearless courage.

> LIFE IS NOT A MATTER OF HOLDING GOOD CARDS, BUT SOMETIMES PLAYING A POOR HAND WELL.
> –JACK LONDON[19]

As you contemplate your own life to get to the bottom of who you are today, use whatever method works best for you. It might help to draw a mind map[20] or create a collage rather than write down your responses to the questions above. Make the process your own. Let this exercise shine light on where you came from, why you are who you are today, and potential platforms for action on social and environmental issues. Highlight whatever seems right to you.

Afterward, ask yourself three more questions:

- **What did you learn about yourself?**

- **What are your roots to the land and/or your community and how do these roots support you in standing up and speaking up in a unique way?**

- **How have your core values already been tested?**

It might be helpful to journal about your answers to these questions. As I discovered by writing down my Sunshine story earlier in this chapter, journaling often leads to fresh insights. Besides reflecting on your life and tracing your roots, another way to develop the power within you is to better understand your inner nature. And who better than Mother Nature to help with that?

TAP THE POWERS OF NATURE

Tuning in to nature does wonders for us because it is another way of tapping into our roots—our deepest roots of all. These roots were formed as humans developed in relation to their environment on this planet thousands and even millions of years ago. When we spend time in nature or among natural things like trees and shrubs or gardens, we can reap healthful benefits. Scientists such as E. O. Wilson have helped us learn we have an innate affinity to other living things. This is called *biophilia*.[21] Just looking out a window on a natural setting or garden has the power to affect our mood, lower our blood pressure, and improve our concentration.[22]

I encourage you to learn more about the science related to human-nature connections. Some resources are suggested.[23, 24, 25, 26] Our environmental connections represent our most basic heritage of all. Sure, most of us recognize our cultural or family heritage, but our environmental heritage provides essential building blocks for life—air, water, food, and shelter.

WE ARE LINKED TO NATURE FOR LIFE.

Even though we are linked to nature for life, many people today do not live with a sense of close connections to their natural environment. With more modern conveniences, supermarkets and crowded cities, we don't interact as much with nature as our grandparents and great-grandparents once did.

You might ask, "Why does this matter if we live more removed from nature?" Because this distance from our roots to the land leaves us less whole and less wholly committed to caring for the Earth. When we distance ourselves from nature, we distance ourselves from solutions to environmental problems. We also deprive ourselves of the gifts nature has to offer us—great sources of knowledge, strength and centering power.

In order to get connected or reconnected with our natural environment, it often takes a deliberate effort. We must purposefully seek experiences with nature or in natural settings. While there is no separating us entirely from nature because of the building blocks of life mentioned above, there are ways to bring nature's benefits forward in our lives. Meaningful experiences help us build a relationship with our Earth and help us better understand our planet's magnificence so we will have a greater sense of what will be lost if we don't stand up for it. The same goes for human communities. We do not care about what we do not know. Get to know your own community and it naturally opens your heart to caring more about it and the people who call it, "home."

Many people before us have shared their thoughts on the values of spending time in natural settings and the powers they have gleaned from nature. Below are a few quotes hinting at the wonders. Perhaps you know of other famous quotes? What wonders of nature have you already discovered?

- "In every walk with Nature one receives far more than he seeks." –John Muir[27]

- "Every particular in nature, a leaf, a drop, a crystal, a moment of time is related to the whole, and partakes of the perfection of the whole." –Ralph Waldo Emerson[28]

- "That I am a saner, healthier, more contented man, with truer standards of life, for all my loiterings in the fields and woods, I am fully convinced." –John Burroughs[29]

- "Everything in the universe has a rhythm. It dances." –Maya Angelou[30]

- "A walk in nature walks the soul back home." –Mary Davis[31]

- "Dwell in the beauty of life. Watch the stars and see yourself running with them." –Marcus Aurelius[32]

- "I firmly believe that nature brings solace in all troubles." –Anne Frank[33]

No matter if you live in an urban environment or in the outback, there are countless ways to tap into the wondrous powers of nature. Choose outdoor experiences for the personal challenge. Choose them because they inspire you. As you become more comfortable in nature and the outdoors, you will make more discoveries and receive even more of the benefits nature has to offer. Nature has a way of challenging us which leads to building courage and resilience. You will discover you belong in the grand scheme of things—that you are here for a reason—and you have tremendous value to offer other people and our planet.

Are you already close to nature and comfortable outdoors? Lucky for you! I hope you will share your connections and adventures with others. Unfortunately, this is not the case for many millions of young adults who have had different life experiences. For some, they have been taught their natural environment is to be avoided or feared. For others, the air quality is so polluted they must avoid outdoor activities. Others stay indoors because there are few safe places to go in their immediate neighborhood or their environment is so degraded there is little incentive to be outdoors. This is precisely why empowering more people to stand up for themselves, their community and our planet is so important: *Things need to change.* Everyone needs and deserves access to their environmental heritage. Everyone needs and deserves a healthy way of life on Earth. Things won't change if there aren't change agents like you equipped to take on the challenge for other people who may not be able to stand up for themselves.

> EVERYONE NEEDS AND DESERVES ACCESS TO THEIR ENVIRONMENTAL HERITAGE.

I've noted a few activity ideas below to *zoom out* for a grand view as you tap the powers of nature. Can you think of some others, too?

- Regularly participate in outdoor adventures that immerse you in a natural area or park. Hike, peddle, paddle, climb, snowshoe, ski, and/or camp. These are just a few of many options.

- Seek opportunities to see yourself as part of this amazing planet in our vast galaxy. Experience grandeur. Watch a sunrise or sunset, star gaze, sit still where there is a panoramic vista, attend an astronomy program at an observatory, or take a silent hike through a beautiful place. Let yourself feel a sense of awe.

- Volunteer in a community garden, zoo, nature center, natural history museum, or other place where you can learn and share your enthusiasm.

- Interview a family member about their personal or cultural traditions related to the Earth or local environment. What benefits do they receive from nature and what do they give back? How have their traditions changed over time? If possible, participate in environmental traditions together.

There is also great benefit when you *zoom in* for a close-up perspective on nature. Here are a few ideas to get you started:

> THE LARGER THE ISLAND OF KNOWLEDGE, THE LONGER THE SHORELINE OF WONDER.
> –HUSTON SMITH[34]

- Grow green plants in or around your home or apartment. If you need help knowing how to grow plants, ask someone who has a green thumb or works at a garden center. Let the plants reveal their wonders as you learn to care for them and watch them grow.

- Take up a nature-inspired art. Photography, painting, and writing poetry are a few ideas. If you are musically inclined, compose a song that has a nature theme. The song I wrote years ago for tree planting ceremonies, "With This Tree," is included in the Appendices.

- Care for a pet. Reflect on its adaptations and how it represents another species on Earth. What lessons does it have to teach you or what lessons have you already learned about nature from your pet?

- Read nature-based writings or poetry. My favorite naturalist writer is John Burroughs who lived from 1837 to 1921 in rural New York State. He was a prolific writer and had a cabin in the woods called Slabsides which is now a National Historic Site.[35] John Burroughs was a friend of U.S. President Theodore Roosevelt, John Muir, and Henry Ford, so there were interesting historic encounters shared through his accounts and tales written by others about him. Other wonderful environmental writers are Aldo Leopold, Henry David Thoreau, and Sigurd Olson. Mary Oliver and Robert Service are two of my favorite poets who have used nature for inspiration.

- Go birdwatching. If possible, set up a feeding station or nesting box and monitor them for activity.

- Plant a garden or a tree. Care for it. Watch it change over time. Notice what other species benefit from it.

Take time to do several *zoom out* and *zoom in* activities before you finish this chapter. If you can (or haven't done so already in your life), make them part of your routine. In order to get the most out of each experience, reflect on them. Consider journaling about them, creating a photo gallery, or illustrating them through your favorite art. You might even create a podcast about your discoveries. What have these experiences taught you? How have they changed you? The more you reflect on your nature-based experiences, the more benefits you will receive from them.

Outdoor activities open the door on all kinds of fun and adventure. I have discovered other benefits of spending time outdoors, too. For example, when I have challenged myself on a rigorous hike and achieve my goal, I feel more capable of achieving other goals in my life, too. I have also discovered that when I spend time in natural places, it gives me positive energy, rejuvenates my spirit, and helps me re-center myself so I am prepared for whatever comes next in my life. It helps me put my perspective back on track because I can see more clearly what is significant in the grand scheme of things and what is not. After the loss of a family member, spending time close to nature along with writing about it helped me overcome my tremendous grief. Each one of us has special needs in our lives. Nature often has a way of helping us address those needs on our own terms if we open ourselves up to letting it happen.

BE SAFE AND LEAVE NO TRACE

I would be remiss in urging you to get outside and immerse yourself in nature if I didn't mention safety and challenge you to reduce your environmental impacts. Whether you are planning an outdoor adventure or exploration in an urban area or in a remote natural area, be prepared and plan for safety and the weather. Tell others where you are going and when you plan to return. Don't depend solely on cell phones for the maps you may need. Build your skills and knowledge before you go. Consider having someone join you who is knowledgeable about the environmental setting and activity you plan to do. Bring water. Consider joining a group led by an expert guide if you are new to an outdoor pursuit or wilderness area. Respect your capabilities and the capabilities of your partners on every adventure. Please do your best to leave no trace behind you.

LET NATURE TEACH YOU

Over my lifetime, I've learned so many valuable lessons from Mother Nature! Please allow me to share a few that have been written into a poem after a hike in the woods. I had been stressed about something and was walking in a daze down the trail. I became aware of a Monarch butterfly (*Danaus plexippus*) flitting from branch to branch in front of me as if it was leading me. The butterfly drew my attention away from stressful thoughts circling in my mind and brought me back to being in the present moment. It awoke me and gave me new perspectives which helped me get over my troubles. Before I got home from my walk, this poem was mostly written:

With a Monarch's Grace

With a Monarch's grace

> *let me grow to love my own ugliness as I go through life's metamorphoses*

> *let me wear my boldly colored cloak without fear*

> *let me brave the ride as the fragrances of life and prevailing winds guide me*

> *let me speak volumes without whispering a word*

With a Monarch's grace

> *let me accept that it's right to rest when dewdrops are heavy*

> *trusting that I will know when it is time for lift-off*

> *let me learn to appreciate life's colorful sweetness*

> *taking time for long drinks of the bounty*

> *let me handle daily zigs and zags with elegance—no matter how strong the winds*

> *let me gather with friends when it feels instinctively right to do so*

With a Monarch's grace

> *let me trust my internal compass for direction*

> *let me chase a dream as high as it takes to catch it and…*

> *let me become all I am capable of becoming as a gentle being in the gardens of this Earth*

—⁓—

BECOME NATURALLY EMPOWERED

Lessons from nature are always there for us. No matter how young or old we are. No matter what our abilities or disabilities may be. No matter where we live or what our personal situation may be. As we seek to learn new lessons and grow through our nature-based experiences, we also grow a transformational power within. As mentioned earlier in this chapter, the science is well-established about how nature can help our mental and physical health. But the power of nature lies in so much more than the research. Nature literally grounds us. It sustains us. It is who we are. What we discover in nature is ourselves. When we know our inner selves well, we are more balanced and confident. This opens us up to receiving one of the greatest gifts we can receive from Mother Nature: *We become naturally empowered.* We trust we are capable. We trust we are ready. We trust we are brave enough to face whatever strong winds blow our way.

When we are empowered, we recognize authority granted to us. In the case of environmental issues, being a citizen of the Earth grants us all the authority we need to rightfully stand up for our planet and ourselves. In the case of social issues, being a member of the community affected by those issues grants us all the authority we need for our right to take a stand.

> BEING A CITIZEN OF THE EARTH GRANTS US ALL THE AUTHORITY WE NEED TO RIGHTFULLY STAND UP FOR OUR PLANET AND OURSELVES.

It's time to take the *Courage and Confidence Self-Assessment* again. No peeking at your past answers. Let's see if anything has changed after you traced your roots and tapped some natural wisdom.

	1 Strongly Disagree	2 Disagree	3 Neutral	4 Agree	5 Strongly Agree
I know what I stand for.					
I have courage.					

I know where my courage comes from.					
I am confident I know my strengths.					
I am confident I know my weaknesses.					
I know how to restore my confidence when it is shaken.					
I am capable of being an agent for change.					
I am empowered to take on any challenge I set my mind to accepting.					

Continue making discoveries about your personal, cultural and environmental roots and you will continue to grow your courage and confidence. This is what I call "a journey of a lifetime" because the growing never stops. As we broaden our experiences and challenge ourselves on our journey, we become even more sure of ourselves and our capabilities. This further enhances the nature of power within us. What a wonderful and enriching cycle!

More courage and confidence mean you stand with greater power as a citizen of the Earth. *Are you ready?*

3

THE NATURE OF POWER AROUND YOU

YOUR PLUG-INS, YOUR PEOPLE

When you plug into your local community and your global community, you may see movements are already underway and you are not alone in wanting to make changes happen. This may give you "shoulders to stand on" or "arms to link with" in helping to support you in taking actions to bring about desired changes. Alternatively, those movements or directions may be counter to the ones you desire, or you may find an absence of attention to the matter of your concern altogether. No matter which situation you discover, there is strength in finding and joining with others who share your desires for change and can help you achieve your goals. Let me share a story to illustrate how being empowered can be life-changing and world-changing. First, I need to offer a bit of historical background:

The *Iron Curtain* was the name for a boundary imposed between 1945 when World War II ended and 1991 when the Cold War ended. It was created and enforced by Russia to separate itself and the countries it influenced from neutral Western European countries or those countries influenced by the United States. Russian-controlled countries in existence in Western Europe at that time found themselves shut off by a political boundary or wall. These countries included East Germany, Czechoslovakia, Poland, Hungary, Romania, Bulgaria, and Albania. The wall was a barrier that separated people, countries, and ideas. In some places like Berlin, Germany, it was a physical barrier. In other places, it was an ideological one. News and other information behind the wall were censored. Other freedoms of people and society were also limited behind the curtain. [36] When I lived in Germany from 1983-1986 and 1990-1993, my German friends shared stories about how their families had been separated because the wall was built between them. They were literally cut off from each other's lives.

I remember visiting Czechoslovakia as part of a tour in 1986. We moved past the guard tower and through a nervous control point for our bus to enter the country and visit Plzen. Air pollution left a brown cloud hanging over the land. Everything was dingy. There was a stench in the air. It was hard to breathe. Soot from burning brown coal made the cobblestone slippery to walk on. There were few trees. Few people were seen anywhere. Store shelves were nearly empty. It was a bleak place—the most depressing community I had ever experienced. The suppression of freedom was palpable.

Now moving ahead with the story:

I was the keynote speaker on the subject of caring for the Earth at the World Association of Girl Guides and Girl Scouts conference in Sonthofen, Germany, in 1992. (Participants in the Girl Scout movement in countries outside of the United States are called Girl Guides.) There is a network of 150 countries across the world that make up the World Association of Girl Guides and Girl Scouts. This conference created an opportunity to bring women and girls together from many countries.

At this point in the story, you might ask: *What can be more benign than a youth movement to engage young people—girls in the case of Girl Scouting and Girl Guiding—in making their communities and their world a better place?*

The Iron Curtain had just come down. Part of it was dismantled because it had been damaged in a storm and was too expensive to repair and replace. Other parts of the physical wall were falling into disrepair. Risking their lives, people behind the wall began flowing through borders to leave communism behind. Others began tearing down the physical wall in Berlin. People in many places demonstrated in the streets and demanded freedom.[37] After almost fifty years of separating families, countries and ideas, the Iron Curtain became a thing of the past.

RECOGNIZE THE POWER OF PEOPLE AND NETWORKS

Girl Guides from behind the former Iron Curtain—Poland, Hungary, Russia and Czechoslovakia—attended the international conference for the first time in nearly a half a century. Seeing them in their unique Girl Guiding uniforms from their respective countries and hearing them speak freely changed my life forever. They told stories about how they had kept Girl Guiding alive in their countries behind the Iron Curtain by doing it underground—without being detected by the communist government in control at the time. Girl Guiding represented freedom to these citizens. If they had been caught, they said there would have been serious punishments. They had, in fact, risked their lives to keep Girl Guiding alive in their families, communities, and countries.

You might ask why did it become such a risk to participate in scouting programs behind the Iron Curtain? Why would government leaders care? Because there is power in groups of people assembling around a common idea.

> THERE IS POWER IN GROUPS OF PEOPLE ASSEMBLING AROUND A COMMON IDEA.

Because there is power in people who build knowledge, skills, and networks. Because the freedom of assembly, of demonstration, of developing a unified voice are some of the greatest powers of all. Furthermore, the power of women elevated through Girl Guiding was also seen as a threat.

Many of us might not consider Girl Scouting or Girl Guiding to be acts of defiance against the establishment because the mission is summed up simply: to empower girls and women. As this story illustrates, people who are connected and empowered can be seen as a threat to controlling authorities who want to keep people down. Empowerment is about being free to stand up for what you believe in. It is the stuff from which change is made.

Can you think of other times recently or historically when empowered people stood up together and helped to make change happen together? The Polish, Czechoslovakian, Russian, and Hungarian Girl Guides show us that empowerment was, for them, worth risking everything. What do you think?

When you plug into what's happening with the issues around you and tap available resources around you, there is no telling what you can accomplish. Develop partners to widen your circle and you can build an even stronger collective voice for impact like people did for Earth Day 1970. Let's delve into that topic a little bit more with an Earth Day 1990 story this time.

CONNECT WITH OTHERS TO INCREASE IMPACT

In 1989 and 1990, while my husband was attending the U.S. Army Academy of Health Science in San Antonio, Texas, I had the opportunity to be the Program Director for the San Antonio Area Council of Girl Scouts. Fresh out of graduate school, I was eager to take my passion for environmental education to this council of about 3,000 members. My master's thesis was about to be published by the Girl Scouts of the USA for worldwide distribution in their new book and contemporary issues program entitled *Earth Matters: A Challenge for Environmental Action*.[38] It would be launched just in time for the 20th Anniversary of Earth Day 1990. One of my job assignments was to develop our council's role in a special event on Earth Day. We would join other community organizations in a public celebration in San Pedro Park. After brainstorming with others, our project became "Hands-On Earth Peace." This was a project that would engage people before, during, and after the event. Let's use it as an example of how to tap into the power around us to increase awareness on issues that matter to us. Here's how it went:

On donated old shower curtains, upholstery scraps, and other waterproof materials, we asked people to trace the shape of their hand and cut out the shape. Then, we had them write their wish for "Earth Peace" in indelible ink on their cut-out. We didn't want the ink to wash off if it rained or if the ground was wet in San Pedro Park during our Earth Day event. Their hand shape with their wish written on it was stapled to the next person's hand shape and wish. As each hand was connected to the next, it created an interesting chain representing a diversity of people and wishes. There were various colors, shapes and sizes of hands in the chain. Wishes were represented in a diversity of symbols, languages, writing or printing styles with ideas ranging from "Save the Whales" to "Everyone would be loved like me" or "Clean water for everyone."

We began growing the Hands-On Earth Peace chain before the event by having Girl Scout troops bring in their own chains to be linked with the chains of other troops. On the day of the event, our goal was to lay the starting chain of wishes for Earth Peace on the ground and grow it around the park as we added the hands and wishes of others who showed up for the Earth Day 1990 celebration. By the end of the day, we wanted to complete the circle in front of the park stage where a closing ceremony would be held. We knew it would take thousands of hands to do it—and a lot of teamwork.

At our Hands-On Earth Peace booth in the park that day, people made their hand cut-out then followed the chain as it snaked through the park until they found girls standing by with staplers ready to add another hand and wish to the end of the chain.

At 4 p.m., we achieved our Hands-On Earth Peace goal! With nearly 7,000 hands and wishes, we joined the ends of the chain together as part of a final closing ceremony. It was an awesome thing to see—how it looked like a whole planet of ideas for a better world. After a few words from speakers, we joined together with a song I had composed called *For Mother* which was accompanied on guitar. (A copy of the music is provided in the Appendices.) We also invited participants to go see "their" Hands-On Earth Peace chain which would be displayed after the event in libraries, schools and other community venues. It was our way of continuing to promote awareness of Earth Day 1990 and our visions for a better world.

An estimated 10,000 people (per the local media) attended the Earth Day 1990 event that day in San Antonio. Media coverage was exceptional, featuring Hands-On Earth Peace in numerous photos. It was noted by reporters as one of the neatest activities going on during the whole event.

This activity illustrates how partnering with others can increase impact. We could, for example, have had our booth by the same name and simply showed up with our chain of hands and wishes and talked about our project with people who stopped by. Instead, we literally opened up the circle for greater awareness and created an unforgettable opportunity to engage more people. This gave us far more impactful results.

MAXIMIZE THE POWER AROUND YOU

Of course, everyone wants to make their efforts as worthwhile as possible. I've created a checklist of eight questions to help you consider how you can maximize the power around you. Use the *Impact Checklist* to see how you've covered all the bases as you plan for taking action.

Impact Checklist
1. What is your issue or opportunity?
2. Who are the players and where are the connections?
3. How can you make your stand in a unique way?
4. Who are your current or potential partners to make it happen?
5. How can you be more inclusive?
6. What resources, networks, or technologies do you need or want to tap?
7. How can you spread the word, create a wider impact, or create a more lasting impact?
8. What do you believe will be the future or potential future impact(s) of your project?

Let's use the example of the Earth Day 1990 activity above and plug it into the checklist to help you understand the opportunities the checklist provides to guide your planning:

1. **What is your issue or opportunity?** *We needed to choose an environmental issue for our booth at the Earth Day 1990 event. Other organizations would also choose theirs. We coordinated ahead of time with other booth participants to make sure we had well-represented coverage of the theme. Girl Scouts didn't want to choose a single issue; we wanted a more holistic concept and chose to focus on peace in the world or what "Earth Peace" might look like.*

2. **Who are the players and where are the connections?** *We needed to involve girls from age five through age eighteen as well as adults from a diversity of perspectives, ability levels and backgrounds. The connections came through the San Antonio Area Council of Girl Scouts and expanded out to include their families and the whole community.*

3. **How can you make your stand in a unique way?** *We created a means for every participant to be actively involved and to express their unique perspective. Troops included the hands-on activity in their troop meetings prior to Earth Day which gave an opportunity for age appropriate preparations and discussions.*

4. **Who are your current or potential partners to make it happen?** *The troops were current partners. Potential partners included business and individual donors of materials for the project. Earth Day 1990 attendees at San Pedro Park were also potential partners and we engaged them throughout the event. Whether they stayed for a short while or for the whole day, there was a way to participate. By making the activity stand out, the media didn't miss it in the sea of other activities happening during the event. We wanted the media to partner with us to help us spread the word about our project, our council, and Earth Day.*

5. **How can you be more inclusive?** *We prepared for involving thousands of others by having the materials available for them to join our hands-on activity. We talked it up at the event and made announcements inviting the public to join us in trying to reach our goal of making the ends of the chain meet in front of the park stage by 4 p.m. for the closing ceremony and music. There was a lot of anticipation and excitement. It became a beautiful and diverse garland of wishes for peace in our world. We broke it into smaller pieces after the event to display segments around our community. This made it more inclusive as we reached out to others who were not able to attend the event.*

6. **What resources, networks, or technologies do you need or want to tap?** *We planned to make sure we had enough resources for the activity. We had cut out some extra hand shapes ahead of time for those who didn't have time to trace and cut their own. This way they could just add their own wish to the chain. During the day, we networked with event participants to invite them to get involved. We also used the public address system at the park to reach out and encourage people to participate. If it was to happen today, we would announce our event on social media, provide regular progress reports through live feeds, and encourage people to come out to the event and join us. We had people with cameras documenting the event. The fact that I was a singer with a guitar and an original song fitting the event theme added an opportunity to tap a unique and creative resource to wrap up the event.*

7. **How can you spread the word, create a wider impact, or create a more lasting impact?** *After the event, we displayed segments of our hand chain around the community with some information about our organization, the Hands-On Earth Peace activity, and Earth Day 1990.*

> *It was a great way to spread the word and create wider impact.*

8. **What do you believe will be the future or potential future impact(s) of your project?** *Many people do not visualize their desired future without prompting from others. This activity prompted them to clarify their own values and publicly announce their wish for Earth Peace. When people "state" a dream or vision, it can be a first step toward making it a reality. Our hope is the activity and event reinforced the concept for the girls and others that by widening the circle to achieve a common goal, it can be more fun and magnify their impact. Maybe some people discovered their wish for Earth Peace was also wished by others. When people realize they are not alone in dreaming their dream, it can be a game changer because there is greater hope that it can happen.*

Let's stop there. Do you see how this checklist will challenge you to expand your thinking as you plan to take a stand on an issue? Do you see how it prompts you to plug into different partners and resources to help you broaden your potential impact?

Another useful planning tool to help you focus on tapping the power around you is to draw a map starting with you and your issue at the center. Spiraling outward from there, brainstorm to include additional people, partners and resources you believe will help you expand your reach and potential for impact. Then, see if you can make it happen!

> BELIEVE YOU CAN AND YOU'RE HALFWAY THERE.
> –THEODORE ROOSEVELT[39]

DIVERSIFY TO ADD SIGNIFICANCE

Let's use the Hands-On Earth Peace concept to illustrate another important point. Imagine two chains of hand cut-outs—one as I described it above and one that was made of uniform hands all cut from the same stencil. Which chain do you think would make the strongest statement or have the most powerful impact overall? The more diverse chain of hands, of course! Tiny hands, large hands, delicate hands, hands with short fingers, pudgy hands, and disfigured hands added to the message that no matter what walk of life, what age, what ability, everyone had a vision for a better world. Just as it is in the natural world when diversity adds significance, interest and resilience, so it is with your cause and community. When you can unify diverse peoples and perspectives around your issue of concern, you will have a more significant, interesting and longer lasting impact.

—⁂—

Referring to the story earlier in this chapter, the Polish, Czechoslovakian, Russian, and Hungarian Girl Guides practiced scouting underground because it was a freedom they were not willing to give up for themselves or their children under the communist regime behind the Iron Curtain. Though there were risks, they secretly connected with others who shared a common vision. *They were empowered.* No one, no political system, no threat would get in the way. They made great sacrifices to keep their dreams alive.

What about you? What is your dream for a brighter future on this planet? How are you working to keep it alive? Who shares your dream? When you find them and connect with them, you will discover a pool of strength. And that is how you tap the nature of power around you.

—⁂—

I returned to Plzen, Czechoslovakia in 1992. The Iron Curtain had fallen a year earlier. What a difference there was compared with my previous visit! I no longer slipped on sooty cobblestone. People were interacting with each other in the streets. There was color everywhere. Stores had supplies. And rebirth was in the air.

In the next chapter, we'll explore some of the action strategies and methods you may want to consider as you develop a plan of action on your social or environmental issue. Whether you are standing up alone or teaming with other people to magnify your voice, there are some important things you can do to improve your chances of success. Turn the page. *Let's move closer to making a positive difference in your community and our world!*

4

MAKING CHANGE HAPPEN

In order to make change happen, you must build your knowledge base related to your issue or opportunity. It is essential to get down to the facts and verify them using several legitimate sources of information. Try to get information from more than one angle or side on the issue. For example, let's say your idea for reducing air pollution in your community is to increase the number of people using a bicycle instead of a car as a regular mode of transportation. You will need to find out not only why people do not bicycle to work or school, but also why other people do. Both bicycling perspectives will help you determine the difference makers—barriers for those who don't and supports for those who do commute by bicycle. Seek out firsthand sources of information. In this example, you might begin by conducting interviews in certain neighborhoods to narrow the focus.

Then, try to look wider at the issue or opportunity. Enhance your understanding of it. For example, are there transportation studies to provide data on the numbers of commuters who bicycle in your community compared to other similar communities? How does your community measure up? Does your community have safe bicycle routes to schools and job sites of major employers? Are there bike racks on buses for longer commutes? Do people know this and know how to use the bus system? Are there road designs that the bicycling public and other users of the road prefer because they are safer? Are bicycle racks available and convenient outside school and work sites? Analyze the information you gather. What can you do to make a difference? Can you find a way to address root causes and support potential solutions?

CLARIFY YOUR SCOPE AND DEFINE SUCCESS

As you consider which action(s) to take, you might need to do more research to refine or narrow your scope. For example, if you want to try to improve the bicycling routes and the availability of racks, you will need to do related research to pinpoint the players, potential partners, and resource organizations connected to your strategy. Perhaps, there is a bicycling club that is already working on the issue. Can you verify they are making a positive difference and then find a way to support their actions? Or, can you raise awareness of your interest in working on this issue and recruit others to join you?

No matter what, being clear about the scope of your initiative is important in giving you a chance to make a meaningful impact on your issue. If your scope is too broad, it may diminish the value of your actions. If your scope is too narrow, it may prevent you from making a positive difference on the issue. The more clearly you define your scope, the more clearly you will be able to define the concrete steps you will need to take on the path to making changes happen. Also, the more clearly you understand your scope, the more clearly you will be able to define what "success" looks like so you know when you get there!

If your issue is local, your root causes or opportunities for solutions may be local—or they may not be. For example, using the bicycling issue above in a community in the United States, imagine you have determined you want to focus on improving road design (such as adding bicycle lanes). Looking into it, you will discover some roads are

DEFINE YOUR SCOPE CLEARLY.

managed locally. That is, decisions about changes to those roads are local decisions made by public officials in local towns, villages, cities and the local county. For other roads, decisions may be made at a higher level of government such as the state level.

GAUGE YOUR READINESS FOR ACTION

How will you know you are ready to stand up on a specific issue? The *Individual Readiness Checklist* below will help you determine where you are clear and where you may need to do additional work before you begin. As you assess your readiness to take action, you will see how it builds on your *Courage and Confidence Self-Assessment* from Chapter 2. Ideally, when you "agree" or "strongly agree" with every item on the checklist, you will be ready to act effectively on an issue that matters to you. Rate your readiness on this scale:

Individual Readiness Checklist	1 Strongly Disagree	2 Disagree	3 Neutral	4 Agree	5 Strongly Agree
I understand my chosen issue well because I have researched it.					
I have narrowed my scope appropriately so I can be more effective.					
I know what I stand for on the issue.					
I have courage to stand up on the issue.					
I know where my courage on the issue comes from.					
I know my strengths on the issue.					

I know my weaknesses on the issue.					
I have determined what my method(s) and pathway(s) for action will be.					
I have determined my timeline.					
I know how I will review or evaluate my actions so I can identify ways to adjust and improve.					
I have determined what my measure(s) of success will be.					

I have the resources I need to be an agent for change on this issue.					
I am confident in my knowledge and abilities to bring about change on this issue.					

For some paths to action you choose, it may seem natural to act alone. For other actions, it will make more sense to gather strength in numbers and team up with others around the same cause as we discussed in Chapter 3.

When you team up with others, how will you know you are ready *as a group* to begin taking action? The *Group Readiness Checklist* below will help. Building on the concepts in the *Individual Readiness Checklist* above, it includes team-related perspectives and additional points that must be considered for successful teamwork. Ideally, when your team "agrees" or "strongly agrees" with every item on the checklist, your team will be ready to act effectively as a group.

Group Readiness Checklist	1 Strongly Disagree	2 Disagree	3 Neutral	4 Agree	5 Strongly Agree
We understand our chosen issue well because we have researched it.					
We have narrowed our scope appropriately so we can be more effective.					
We know what our group stands for on the issue.					
We have collective courage to stand up on the chosen issue.					

We know where our courage as a group comes from on the issue.					
Our group is clear about who leads us.					
Our group knows how we will communicate to keep everyone in the loop.					
We are confident we know our group's strengths on the issue.					
We are confident we know our group's weaknesses on the issue.					

We have determined as a group what our method(s) and pathway(s) for action will be and who will do what.					
We have determined our timeline.					
We know how we will review or evaluate our group's actions so we can identify ways to adjust and improve.					
We have determined as a group what our measure(s) of success will be.					

Our group has the resources it needs to be an agent for change on this issue.					
Our group is confident in our knowledge and abilities to bring about change on this issue.					

—⁂—

CHOOSE METHODS FOR ACTION FROM SMILES

How will you know what method(s) or pathway(s) to action are right or best for your plan to tackle the issue you are concerned about? Certainly, it depends on your issue, but it also depends on your goal, scope, comfort level, and resources to pull it off. I have compiled a list of common methods activists use to address social and environmental issues. The list is categorized to create an acronym, SMILES, to help you remember the choices:

S – Serving People and Nature through Hands-on Projects

M – Modeling the Change

I – Influencing Community and Government

L – Litigating for Justice and Change

E – Educating People in Support of Change

S – Standing Up on Consumer Choices

Within these categories, there is something for everyone—no matter who you are or where you live. Let's drill down to look at each of these six categories for action with some examples of each—including some examples from my own life:

Serving People and Nature through Hands-on Projects: Just as its name suggests, this category for action involves being immersed in service to others to make the world a better place. It might be a project created by others or one you organized on your own. It might be a one-time service project or involve you in regular service and support for a cause or organization you believe in. Some examples in this category for action are:

- Planting trees and community gardens.

- Feeding the hungry at a local soup kitchen.

- Doing a streambank restoration project.

- Beautifying a park.

- Working with solid waste authorities to get household hazardous wastes like paint thinner or varnish disposed of properly.

- Doing a citizen science project to gather data about natural resources.

One example of a citizen science project is becoming trained as a stream monitor for a stream in your community, then submitting your data points regularly to an organization such as the Izaak Walton League of America which maintains a database to track water quality trends.[40] There are many other examples of citizen science initiatives going on across the world.[41, 42, 43, 44, 45, 46] This category for action might also include fund-raising for a cause or organization to support your goal. The results of actions taken in this category are often tangible—that is, you can see the difference you are making. Longer-term benefits are possible when projects build new capacities and skills in other people so they can better help themselves going forward. Lasting benefits also result when projects improve the environment.

> YOU ARE HERE TO ENRICH THE WORLD AND YOU IMPOVERISH YOURSELF IF YOU FORGET THE ERRAND.
> –WOODROW WILSON[47]

One of my recent projects to serve people and nature was to share information with my neighbors about an invasive plant that I had recently discovered in our neighborhood—teaching them about it, offering fact sheets I had obtained about the species, and partnering with them to eradicate it from their property.

Modeling the Change: Through this category, you demonstrate through your voice and actions what matters to you. It is a way of living your values—of walking your talk. Ideally, you want others to model your choices, your actions. You may be a silent model, or you may use your example to teach and perhaps persuade others. Some examples in this category for action are:

- Sharing with a neighbor how easy it is for you to do backyard composting of your kitchen scraps.

- Bringing your own reusable plates and silverware to a community picnic while encouraging others to do the same.

- Eating more locally grown foods and having your friends over to share the bounty.

- Using public transportation.

The results are immediate when you "live the changes" you want to see in the world.[48] Results may also be long-term when you adopt and sustain new behaviors and lifestyles—and inspire others to do the same.

One of the ways I model my values is to collect organic waste such as banana peels and eggshells while I am staying at a family member's house where they don't compost table scraps. We keep the scraps in a bag in the freezer. When I leave, I take the bag with me. At home, I add the scraps to the compost in my backyard. I've also brought home organic waste generated in my office at work. Why let organic nutrients for our garden go to waste by throwing them in the garbage?

Influencing Community and Government: This category involves honest and appropriate ways of seeking to influence community leaders and government officials to make policy changes or other adjustments favorable to your issue. The leaders or officials you seek to influence may or may not be elected. Community leaders you might want to influence include those heading up non-profit, business, educational, or religious organizations. They might also be thought leaders or influential people who are organizers in your community or in the wider world. They might be government staff who can help you influence elected government officials. The scope might be local, state, national, or international. Some examples of actions to influence community and government are:

- Providing testimony at a public meeting.

- Communicating with elected officials and their staff to share your views.

- Gathering community leaders together to discuss an issue and collaborate on a solution.

- Expressing your viewpoint publicly through the general media or social media.

- Organizing listening sessions on an issue and presenting your results to policy makers.

- Gathering signatures for a petition.

- Conducting a community survey and sharing results with local leaders.

- Organizing a demonstration.

- Voicing your opinion at a summit.

When I was an elected government official, people influenced me on issues that mattered to them and I influenced them, too. One time, a ten-year-old wrote me a detailed letter about our library and what it meant to have his library located downtown. (We had been considering if we would build a new one somewhere else in the community.) He later testified confidently at a county board meeting on the same issue and made a great impact on everyone. At his young age, he did what many adults have never done in their lifetime: stand up at a government meeting to voice their views to help shape their community's future. I share this story here to encourage you. Speaking up at local government meetings is often as easy as raising your hand and sharing a few thoughts. Having your ideas or concerns written down beforehand will help you speak with more confidence.

There are many ways to exchange ideas and influence government or community leaders besides speaking at public meetings. One time, I asked to be on the agenda of a teen leadership event and got to spend a couple of hours with young adults gathering their ideas for development of our county's first strategic plan. Since these young citizens literally *were* our community's future, their viewpoints were priceless to me and greatly influenced the way I carried on with our countywide strategic planning process. Community and government leaders may be willing to attend your group's meetings, too. Invite them.

The numbers of people and diversity of voices often add strength when seeking to influence community or government changes, so build a strong team. Also, it is important to engage people who are voters in the district of an elected official you want to influence. Results of policy changes can be longer term if the policy remains "on the books" and is enforced. It can be weakened or reversed by whomever is subsequently elected so you must be vigilant (and always exercise your right to vote). Without watchdogs or other people monitoring compliance with a policy change, your efforts may not have a lasting impact. Be sure to address how compliance will be monitored as part of your solution.

Hands-on or "field" activities can also be very helpful when you want to influence others. One citizen invited me to his rural property to show me how water was backing up on his land because of an old town road nearby which needed a culvert improvement. He wanted me to talk to leaders in his town. I did. The culvert improvement was made. Another citizen, a vegetable grower, invited me to his land to teach me about how his farming operation worked and how he irrigated his fields. On many occasions, I used the insights he shared while helping others understand the challenges faced by farmers.

On a different occasion in my own efforts to influence elected leaders at the state level, I organized a "Water Field Day for Legislators." This involved hosting a bus tour with local elected officials, state legislators, media members, area experts in water related fields, and other interested citizens to highlight water science and water-related issues around our county. For example, we stopped at a location where there was a test well used to measure the depth of groundwater in that area. Everyone got to see how water depth data was gathered. We also stopped at a local county park to discuss how pumping millions of gallons of groundwater to irrigate crops was lowering our water table and affecting groundwater-fed lakes and streams. At another stop, we caught macroinvertebrates and shared a stream ecology lesson. Through this field day, we influenced a state legislator who mentioned what she learned at our event when she stood up to explain her vote about a proposed change to Wisconsin's water law at our State Capitol.

A contrasting example was when a family asked me to meet them at their kitchen table with their neighbors to talk about water quality issues in their rural area—just five of us together for a couple of hours. They also wanted to show me the device used to treat their well water at their kitchen tap in order to make it safer to drink.

Perhaps most memorable was when I learned of gaps in serving Hmong Americans in our community and county government. Leaders of the Hmong community met several times with me over a year or so to discuss and address various concerns and issues. Together, we wanted to see what we could do to improve the ways our community and government served them. It was very exciting to learn when one member of our work group decided to run for public office herself! She won the election and became a county board supervisor, a legislator in our local community, who went on to break cultural barriers and more directly serve members of her Hmong community in her elected role. Even more fantastic was the fact that another member of the Hmong community followed her lead and ran for a position on a local school board. She was also elected. What began in our discussions around a common table led to empowering one who empowered another, and the rest is history.

I don't want you to feel intimidated by elected officials. They are regular people. They may be more well-known than you are, but they are people just like you. There is no reason to be nervous. As the above examples illustrate: Reach out to them. Invite them to experience your perspective firsthand. Teach them. You may be surprised at where it can take you on your way to finding solutions on your issue. Don't get discouraged if you don't get the attention you think your concern rightfully deserves. Keep trying. Strengthen your team and approach. And remember, if you live in a democratic society, voting is one of the most powerful ways to evaluate the performance of elected officials! Don't miss voting in *any* election. They all affect you.

Be careful about political action committees (PACs) which support certain candidates or issues. Their names are often deceiving! Some PAC names make themselves sound like they care about the environment or are heroes on community issues when in fact, they are not. They have their own agenda and have chosen a name or slogan to try to make themselves look good and fool people into joining them. Think *propaganda* and *misconception* until you drill down to prove them otherwise! Actions always speak louder than words, so find out about their track record. Don't just blindly follow their claims without doing your homework first or they may lead you down a path contrary to your own values.

> DON'T MISS VOTING IN ANY ELECTION BECAUSE THEY ALL AFFECT YOU.

When tackling widespread or planet scale problems or issues, it will require influencing numbers of communities and governments. Don't let this challenge turn you away. Start where you are with local efforts. Widespread issues are often very serious matters affecting your future. This makes them worth an investment of your time and effort. Sometimes, as we get key leaders or governmental units on board, others follow suit creating a cascading effect and the chance for making tremendous headway on the issue.

Litigating for Justice and Change: This action category involves being part of a lawsuit to seek a resolution on an issue through a court of justice or tribunal. Some examples are:

- Becoming directly involved in a legal case.

- Filing a petition for an injunction to suspend an activity that you must prove will cause irreparable harm to people and/or the environment if it is not halted immediately.

- Participating in a tribunal or mediation which specializes in your area of concern to try to resolve a legal dispute.

- Joining one or more organizations seeking justice through a court of law on your issue.

Some organizations make it their mission to fight for change through a legal process. It may take quite a long time, but the results can be powerful and set precedents which shape future decisions—not only the decisions made in your case. Certainly, litigation requires extraordinary expertise and resources, but don't count it out as a choice for action on your issue!

Be cautious of misleading organizational or foundation names that sound like they stand for justice or environmental or community causes when in fact they do not. Once again, think *propaganda* and *misconception* until you drill down and prove them otherwise. Find out the facts about organizations *from other sources, not just their own websites and their other communications.* Look into their track record and actions before you support them!

Educating People in Support of Change: This category for action involves sharing information to increase awareness of the facts about an issue to teach others and help them learn how they can become part of a solution. Some examples of actions in this category are:

- Teaching business owners how to reduce waste in their place of business and why it is good for business to do so.

- Creating an educational video series for social media to encourage your peers to shop at a farmer's market for locally grown fruits and vegetables and challenging them to take the "I buy local" challenge you have designed.

- Delivering an educational program on pollinators for youth at a school in preparation for a community service project when you help them plant a pollinator garden.

- Hosting a backyard habitat workshop during a special community event.

Helping people build their awareness and knowledge about an issue are good starting places, but you will also need to make sure they have the *skills* for action. What will they need to be able to *do* to be successful in taking the specific actions you invite them to take? Here are some skills you may need to build in your target audience for the examples of educational projects listed above:

Educational Project	*Examples of Skills Needed*
Teaching business owners about waste reduction.	How to organize a waste reduction program in a workplace.
Promoting a *buy local* campaign among peers.	How to shop at a farmer's market.
Teaching about pollinators.	How to do a pollinator inventory.
Hosting a backyard habitat workshop.	How to plant and care for trees given away to workshop participants.

Here are a few other examples of skills you might need to build in your target population as you work through other kinds of educational projects:

- How to register to vote.

- How to communicate effectively with elected officials.

- How to make safe alternatives to household cleaning chemicals.

- How to properly sort waste for recycling in your community.

- How to gather and submit data to be a citizen scientist.

Get the idea? Let the question of "How?" lead you to identify the skills you may need to help your target audience prepare for action.

Often, informal ways of assessing the knowledge and skills gaps are all you need. You might ask your participants on the spot what they know or need. Or, you might let them self-select from options you provide to meet their own needs. For example, you might include a template for people to use in writing to their legislator. Participants will take the template if they feel they need it.

If you want a more formal way of assessing the knowledge and skills of your target audience, you can conduct a short pre-survey. Pre-surveys allow you to find out what your audience knows about the topic and what they may need to be ready to participate as a change maker. Another formal method is to gather a focus group of your intended audience to ask for their input and feedback before you develop the program.

The more you break down barriers that might otherwise get in the way of action, the more results you can expect to achieve from your educational and outreach efforts. Though certainly not required, incentives can invite people to break down barriers for themselves. For example, if you teach a composting workshop and give participants a discount on the purchase of a compost bin for their backyard because you arranged for the discount from a business partner, your chances of helping them take their education to action will increase significantly. As another example, imagine you are conducting an educational program urging more people to use public transportation. You could offer free bus tokens. The point is to make it as easy as possible for people to get involved.

Educational outreach projects may rely on face-to-face communication with individuals or groups. They may also rely on communicating through social media, news media, the internet, or even billboards. You might try to persuade people to change their routine, donate to a cause, make different choices, or vote a certain way. The sky is the limit. It is all about educating *for action*—not just information sharing.

There are important considerations when you seek to focus on children and youth with your education efforts. The best educational programs for children and youth engage them in age, ability, and culturally appropriate ways. Involve teachers, youth leaders, and families when you can. It may be appropriate to share your personal experiences and why you feel compelled to stand up on your issue. However, stop short of telling them how they *should* feel or what they *should* do because they need the opportunity to discover those things on their own.

No matter if you are educating adults or youth to support change, results are sometimes hard to gauge because you may not be able to see those results immediately. A quick pre-survey of a few questions before your program followed by a repeat of the same survey at the end of your program can give you a sense of what people learned. You might ask adult participants to express their commitment to change their behavior or make a pledge to take a certain action after you have finished your outreach to them. Or, you might ask people to self-report the changes they make over time—perhaps on a certain social media site. Benefits can be lifelong when you help people change their ways! That's why it is so important to break through barriers which prevent action.

The excitement of this category is what I call the "multiplier effect." This is what happens when your education equips and inspires other people and they take actions of their own. It multiplies or magnifies your impact—not just for this one issue this one time—but potentially for many other times and in many other ways, too.

Standing Up on Consumer Choices: This action strategy is one with more power than most people may realize. It is about exercising your power as a consumer of goods and services. Everything you buy or avoid buying is the same as speaking your mind. When you buy a product or service, it is the same as saying you approve of it and you approve of the practices of its makers or providers. Buying a product or service is a way of showing your support for a business. Alternatively, when you avoid buying a product or service even when you can afford to pay for it, you send a message it is not needed, not preferred, or not worthy of your support. Examples of actions in this SMILES category are:

- Doing your homework before you buy anything so you can make an informed decision.

- Boycotting a business with unhealthy products or practices.

- Recognizing businesses being good stewards in your community.

Each of us has an ecological footprint which measures the annual demand we place on global natural resources because of our way of life. Not only is it about what we consume and how much we consume, but about processing the waste we produce.[49, 50] The greater our footprint, the more we demand from our planet. Our consumer choices go hand-in-hand with our lifestyle choices. Together, they figure greatly into how much pressure we place on our planet's finite resources. The results of standing up on consumer choices are passed along through the sales figures tracked by businesses. The more people involved in making the same consumer choice such as using a more environmentally friendly product or boycotting a company doing bad business on our planet, the greater our chances for more immediate impact and change.

On the way to developing your best action plan, consider all SMILES categories, then zero in on the most appropriate action(s) for your issue. This way, you'll be sure not to overlook a better strategy for action than the first one you thought of. Don't feel like you need to stick within one of the action categories, either. Challenge yourself (and your team) to review the choices within and across SMILES strategies. Integrate them if you can. Then, develop a well-rounded, concrete plan with a clear idea of how you will define success. Make sure it is a plan with constructive and respectful steps for moving forward as opposed to simply demeaning those with differing views. When you can, affirm what is already working, then build on it. This reinforces a common direction and will increase your momentum. The readiness checklists presented earlier in this chapter are tools to help you get there. The SMILES categories will help you stay on track for getting results.

As we wrap up this chapter, I want to offer a story with an example of an action project which began with a cultural divide and a recycling challenge and ended up enhancing international relations and forming lifelong friendships. Perhaps, your action plan will help you discover whole new horizons and friendships, too!

LET COLLABORATION LEAD YOU FORWARD

In 1991, I was hired to work for the U.S. Army Environmental Office of the 98th Area Support Group in Würzburg, Germany. I had joined my husband in Würzburg while he was serving a military assignment. I became the coordinator of the Separate or Recycle Trash (SORT) Program, a new solid waste program serving about 60,000 Americans living in military communities around Würzburg.

Germany was (and still is) advanced in the field of solid waste management with strict laws and norms related to reducing waste and recycling. Würzburg's German communities did a superb job of sorting their waste. They had adjusted to those laws and practices in their homes and communities. In contrast, military service men and women and their families living in the Würzburg area came from many different communities prior to living in Germany. They didn't necessarily know the German laws. Communities in the U.S. and around the world where they had lived before coming to Würzburg didn't recycle the same things. There were cultural and language barriers also preventing Americans from understanding German laws and norms. In short, we, Americans, were making a lot of mistakes with our waste. Without meaning to, we were making it difficult for our host nation to manage its solid waste efficiently and effectively.

Enter the SORT Coordinator—me! One of my jobs as SORT Coordinator was to improve American performance in sorting waste on military installations where many military members lived and worked. I also had the job of reaching out to service men and women and their families living in German neighborhoods.

Some connections were made with our local city officials in solid waste management and at the local university in Würzburg. Before we knew it, we were learning from each other. I taught them about environmental education—a relatively new field of study at the time—and they taught me about host nation laws and practices. I taught them about the Central Wisconsin Environmental Station at the University of Wisconsin-Stevens Point College of Natural Resources, my alma mater, and they taught me about leading edge waste incinerators and community-wide composting programs. I taught them about Earth Day and they taught me about *Umwelt Tag* (World Environment Day celebrated in Germany). Together, we worked to improve the performance of Americans sorting their waste. Together, we worked to try to help our German neighbors become more patient and understanding of Americans learning new systems and ways.

By this time, we had tapped all the SMILES action categories except litigation (thank heaven). We had done waste sorting service projects including a waste assessment on our military installation. We had government officials informed and involved in cooperative ways. We had modeled and educated and tried to help Americans make better consumer choices by avoiding waste when they could.

That's when we began to see there was an even more important opportunity for our partnership—to bring the people of our two countries closer together. The U.S. military had a presence in Germany because it had been invited to be there after WWII. Americans living in Würzburg needed to see themselves as ambassadors because—like it or not, recognize it or not—we were! This was a grand opportunity to act more like guests

> HOW OFTEN I FOUND
> WHERE I SHOULD BE
> GOING BY SETTING
> OUT SOMEWHERE ELSE.
> –R. BUCKMINSTER FULLER[51]

in our host nation. At the same time, some citizens of Würzburg could be better ambassadors of their country and help the Americans feel more welcomed, too.

We needed to build a common understanding and what better way to do that than by celebrating being in it together—sharing one home, one Earth? We decided we would participate in each other's environmental holidays—Earth Day and *Umwelt Tag*. This led to co-founding the first German-American Earth Day in 1991 followed about a month later by celebrating German-American *Umwelt Tag*. Our first German-American Earth Day event brought 150 elementary school children (eight and nine years old) and their teachers together with military officials and City of Würzburg officials at an American school for military families at Leighton Barracks, an Army installation. Seventy-five children were from German schools and seventy-five children were from American schools. We chose third graders because this was the grade when the German children began to learn English in school.

If you would like to learn more about German-American Earth Day, the Appendices include more of the story.

When it was time to participate in *Umwelt Tag* festivities, the American children went to the *Umweltstation Würzburg*, the Environmental Station in the City of Würzburg. This was a place much like a nature center in America where they were immersed in hands-on activities with the German children. German and American dignitaries were once again present.

I never imagined where this collaboration to help Americans sort their waste properly in Würzburg would lead! The German-American Earth Day tradition continued for fifteen years until the military drawdown and American military families were no longer stationed in Würzburg. Not only did we improve solid waste management and recycling in Würzburg, we improved international relations. Not only did we serve U.S. Army communities, but before I left Germany in 1993,

I was asked to make a presentation to the U.S. Navy because they wanted to learn from our model.

RIPPLES MAY BECOME MOVEMENTS

I continue to connect with my German colleagues—Dieter, Bernd, and Helmer (Charly) almost thirty years later. We have developed lifelong friendships and have grown to be part of each other's family. Together, we have written the Afterword of this book and will continue our collaboration as we share *Empowered: One Planet at a Time* across the Earth.

You'll never know where your journey will take you until you get started and let the SMILES categories lead you forward as you develop your plan for action. Once you get going, be ready for an amazing life as a change maker! What starts as a ripple today may become a movement tomorrow. You might shape traditions that last longer than you ever imagined. You might create life-changing and world-changing friendships, too. When we see ourselves as *one* and *in this together,* it changes everything—for the better.

5

GROWING AND SUSTAINING YOURSELF THROUGH ACTION AND SERVICE

YOUR PERSEVERANCE, YOUR PROGRESS, YOUR IMPACTS

If you're going to tackle tough issues to make the future brighter, you need to be able to stay in the game as an agent for change. This means you must know how to sustain yourself for the journey. Let's look at how to track your progress and stay centered as you handle the "zigs and zags" along the way.

You have prepared yourself, chosen an issue you feel passionate about, and developed a plan of action. If your issue requires a team approach, your team is ready. You are about to launch your plan and you might be thinking, "What happens if I (or we) fail?"

The fact is, there is no such thing as failing when you approach your issue with a heart for serving people and our planet. Since

89

Earth is home to us all and everything is connected to everything else—your sincere effort to make the world a better place is commendable. Why should you feel badly for trying if you don't see progress as quickly as you had hoped? You simply dedicated yourself to try to find a way forward to bring about positive changes. It is an admirable thing to do! It may require several attempts. You will never know what works until you try. You will need to stay the course. Giving up is not an option when you consider this is the only planet to call *home*.

Consider Thomas Edison's story: He tested thousands of theories on his way to discovering what worked to invent the electric lightbulb. Through multiple attempts, he learned what didn't work which was just as important as learning what did work.[52] As long as you try to reap the lessons learned, there is no such thing as a failure. Think of it as if you are walking through a maze: When you find a path that doesn't seem to be going where you believe it should be going or you hit a dead end, retrace your steps—that is, learn from what happened—and try a different path next time.

PROGRESS, NOT PERFECTION

My friend, Kari, recently made a presentation about living more lightly on the planet—you know, tips and tricks for reducing the environmental impacts in our daily lives. One example was how she makes her own toothpaste from baking soda, water and a drop of mint extract so she doesn't need to buy nonrecyclable tubes of toothpaste anymore. Another example was how she reduces waste by carrying her own utensils with her wherever she goes to reduce her use of disposable silverware. She talked about taking it one step at a time—establishing a process to change one behavior at a time—to create a routine in our lives. Otherwise, she says, we can become overwhelmed and make no progress at all. Kari's motto was "Progress, Not Perfection!"[53]

The same concept applies here to your actions. *This is about finding a way forward, not about finding a perfect path.* Roll with the changes. Be ready to alter your original course if it seems practical. Don't worry if others do not recognize or appreciate your efforts. John Lennon said, "When you do something noble and beautiful and nobody noticed, do not be sad. For the sun every morning is a beautiful spectacle and yet most of the audience still sleeps."[54]

CELEBRATE WHAT YOU'VE GAINED

Whenever you make a stand for any kind of change, you owe it to yourself to reflect on the process and celebrate what you have gained. Maybe you have gained ground. Maybe you have gained valuable experience. Maybe you have gained confidence. Maybe you have gained partners on your team or support for your cause. Or maybe, you have gained awareness that your effort to drive change is going to be harder and take longer than you first thought! Tracking your progress—even small bits of progress or barely visible changes—can help you persevere. Even when you have gained frustration because the opposition to change is greater than originally thought, perhaps you can also see your frustration is an indicator of how much more deeply you care than you initially knew. These discoveries define progress.

Acknowledge where you got stuck but didn't stay that way, or where you had a breakthrough because you let your creativity help you rise to the challenge. Notice when there was an unexpected turn of events and you maintained your composure despite it all. These acknowledgements highlight areas of growth. They can become sources of energy to propel you forward.

When you only focus on where you are going (as in the next step in your action plan), you may miss the benefits of seeing how far you've come along the way. Pause to reflect on your leadership, your responses, and your lessons learned. This will help you maintain a strong sense of self-growth in the process. Awareness of how you are growing will help you recognize personal progress. This awareness builds your confidence in your abilities as a change maker.

Whatever your wisps of hopeful progress look like, whatever your personal triumphs, whatever do-overs you would like, or whatever the grand and solid advancements on your issue may be: Recognize them. Review them. Own them. Every attempt is a discovery about what works and doesn't work in one place and at one time.

LIVE YOUR JOURNEY AND BECOME CHANGED

Even a few minutes of journaling each week (or regularly on a schedule that suits you best) can reveal the most amazing transformations when you look back at your efforts over time. How do I know? Because it's happened to me! I've read my old notes and reflections and am stunned by how much I have grown since I wrote them. As you explore how you feel about the paths you have chosen and consider your thoughts along the way, you will notice changes taking place as you live your journey. Norman Vincent Peale said, "Change your thoughts and you change your world."[55] Another way to think about it is, "As you seek to change the world, you become changed."

—⁓—

After the Iron Curtain fell, I was invited to travel with a German delegation of teachers, university faculty, and other leaders to bring environmental education to Hungarian teachers in Budapest. The year was 1992. For over forty years, teachers in Budapest had been isolated from the educational advancements taking place across the world—including the fact that there was a new field—the field of environmental education.

I remember digging down deep inside myself as I began to develop my program. Environmental education had a lot to offer them—especially as they were tending to a rebirth of their country. It was (and still is) a valuable tool for engaging young people to achieve educational goals across all subject areas. I was told to expect Hungarian classrooms didn't have many resources and to design strategies requiring minimal supplies.

As the only American in the delegation, not only did I feel the weight of being an ambassador for the field of environmental education born out of Earth Day 1970 in the United States, but also as an ambassador for my country. I would probably be the first American many of the Hungarian teachers had ever met. This was a once-in-a-lifetime opportunity. Naturally, I wanted to do my best.

> WHERE THERE IS GREAT LOVE, THERE ARE ALWAYS MIRACLES.
> –WILLA CATHER[56]

And that's when I realized it: *Before I could teach teachers for a brighter future in Hungary, I first had to feel the brighter future inside myself.* I had to believe I had something of value to offer and that I could make a positive difference. I had to visualize the changes before I could be a successful supporter of change in Budapest. *I grew from the inside out as I became a change maker in our delegation.* We came offering a wellspring of support and resources. We came in the spirit of international friendship and love. We let them know they were not alone. And I was never the same again.

> WHEN I LOOK AT THE EARTH IN PICTURES TAKEN FROM SPACE...I SEE NO BOUNDARIES...I FEEL LIKE A PLANETARY CITIZEN. –SHURLI GRANT, "PLANETARY CITIZENS" IN RAINBOW, AS CITED BY CHRIS HIGHLAND (2004, P. 125)[57]

It will be this way for you, too. You will go through a metamorphosis with every change you make in our world. Laozi, said, "When I let go of what I am, I become what I might be."[58] Just like it was for me, you will experience growth from the inside out.

It is like the caterpillars of Monarch butterflies (*Danaus plexippus*) I picked up on Common Milkweed (*Asclepias syriaca*) last week. I was walking my dog along a country road when a large mower came over the hill toward us. It was a huge machine cutting a wide swath along the road's edge as they do every year at this time—the prime time when the first generation of Monarch caterpillars is maturing on milkweed growing in the sunny ditches. Their parent butterflies had migrated hundreds of miles from the south. Eggs were laid on the first leaves of milkweed, their larval food in Wisconsin at this time of year. Now these Monarch caterpillars—butterflies-to-be—were destined to be killed before my eyes.

The mower was coming right toward us.

I was darned if I was going to watch the mower shred them. In that moment, I began to pick milkweed on which I saw the yellow and black and white striped caterpillars. Remembering an old poem about a man throwing beached starfish back into the sea,[59] I carried the small bouquet home with me. Within a week, one of the caterpillars pupated forming a magical light green colored chrysalis which looked like it had been stitched together with metallic gold thread and studded with tiny golden gems. What an incredible work of art! As I write this, I wait for the orange and black adult butterfly to *eclose* from its chrysalis and take flight.

Through the complete metamorphosis process, the butterfly *lets go* of its former self in order to fly as an adult. The adult butterfly looks nothing like the glossy green pupa from which it matured. The pupa looks nothing like the striped larva (caterpillar) from which it developed. And the yellow, black, and white striped caterpillar looks nothing like the cream-colored egg from which it hatched on a milkweed leaf. Witnessing a Monarch's complete metamorphosis is as incredible as observing our own kind of transformation when we become agents for change in the world. When we live life as empowered people, we are never the same again.

TRACK YOUR PROGRESS

Besides personal growth, what else might progress look like if you haven't yet achieved your complete goal? It might show up as growth in your team's development—areas such as how you have cooperated with each other, how you have established a new way to track your team's actions, or how your team has increased in size with people passionate about making the changes happen. Below, I've listed a few other examples to get you thinking about measures or indicators of progress. Of course, they are dependent on the nature of your social or environmental project.

Category of Action	*Some Possible Indicators of Progress*
Serving People and Nature through Hands-on Projects	• Numbers of people served. • Data collected. • Clean up projects completed. • Numbers of people trained and organized as citizen scientists.

Modeling the Change	<ul><li>Personal actions taken to model change.</li><li>Lifestyle changes made.</li><li>Number of people reached to share your story of "being the change."</li></ul>
Influencing Community and Government	<ul><li>Testimony given at a public meeting.</li><li>Elected officials contacted and engaged on your issue.</li><li>Forums held.</li><li>Community surveys completed.</li><li>Numbers of people registered to vote.</li><li>Votes cast.</li><li>Number of signatures obtained on a petition.</li></ul>
Litigating for Justice and Change	<ul><li>Mediations attended.</li><li>Information gathered to support a legal case.</li><li>Legal cases filed.</li><li>Organizations supported in legal action.</li></ul>

Educating People in Support of Change	• Focus groups held. • Posts shared on social media. • Podcasts launched. • Special events organized. • Press releases distributed. • Number of people served through educational programs you have delivered.
Standing Up on Consumer Choices	• Purchases avoided. • Consumer decisions made in support of businesses with track records aligned with your personal values. • Number of consumers reached about participating in a boycott you have organized.

If you are familiar with logic models which help us develop action plans and evaluation methods,[60] most of the above measures of progress are inputs, outputs, or outcomes on the way to achieving your ultimate desired impacts on your issue of concern. They are much like steppingstones to move your project forward.

It's easy to lose track of the steps you took to address your issue unless you document them. By tracking your progress over time, you will be able to look back and recall the details about what worked and what didn't work so well—important lessons which may serve you on other projects in the future. Documenting your progress will also enable you to reproduce the information for an after-action report or presentation to teach others what you learned and what you accomplished. If you are working with a team, consider holding periodic after-action discussions to highlight and record your team's progress.

USE TOUGH TIMES TO YOUR ADVANTAGE

Most likely, the challenges of making desired changes happen and resolving issues won't be easy and won't come quickly. You might encounter obstacles or painful moments. There might be times when you feel like giving up. We've all felt that way.

During tough times, reflect on your roots as you did in Chapter 2. Why did you choose this issue in the first place? What are your pivot points of courage on the issue? How can you draw strength from those points of courage? What will your future or the future of others look like if you give up rather than push forward with renewed commitment and passion? Who or what is counting on you? Tough times are also great times to seek out a friend or mentor to talk it through. The bottom line is for you to *use tough times to your advantage.*

If tough times seem to draw you inward, let it happen. Reflect. Remember where you came from. Think about role models who courageously faced challenges and persevered. Be still in nature. Trust yourself and how you will "know when it is time for lift-off" per *With a Monarch's Grace* from Chapter 2.

If tough times seem to draw you outward, go outdoors! Follow that flow. Give yourself time and space. Participate in rigorous outdoor activities. Release nervous energy and replace it with greater determination.

Tough times are those times when some of our greatest life lessons are nearest at hand. Open yourself to receive what they can teach you. Rather than struggling against challenges, it helps us move through them more quickly and gracefully when we roll with them and turn them into learning opportunities. Allow yourself time to discern the hidden gifts to be discovered.

—⁂—

A few years ago, I helped to lead a march on our State Capitol in Wisconsin in support of people with disabilities. Their lives were being turned upside down. A critical program, IRIS[61] which gave stability to their daily lives, was at risk of being eliminated. The program helped them match their individual needs with home-based caregiving resources so they could live as independently as possible. The threat of defunding the program was also creating turmoil in the business community. For example, home care agencies with personal care providers were unsure about hiring more staff to meet the needs of people in their communities. Some of them were unsure about staying in business at all if there were no assurances the program funding would continue. If businesses folded during the turmoil, thousands of people receiving their home care services could be stranded without help.

This misguided policy proposal at the state level in Wisconsin had people rightfully up in arms and I joined the fight. Remembering my roots and my mom with significant disabilities in her life, I was clear why this program was worth standing up for.

On that day of the rally, we crowded into a room in the health and human services building where the media was present for some speeches, including my own. When we finished setting the stage on the issue, we marched to the Capitol a few blocks away—cameras rolling for the television news that evening, photos being snapped for social media and newspapers. People walking with canes. People in powered wheelchairs. People pushing loved ones who couldn't power themselves in wheelchairs. People walking with service dogs. Families walking in honor of their loved ones at home. Children, elders, caregivers, business owners, families and elected officials (like me).

When we got to the Capitol, we dispersed to visit our legislators. Unfortunately, some doorways into some legislators' offices were not wide enough to accommodate larger wheelchairs. I was grateful to learn some legislators and their staff took the opportunity to talk with our rally participants in the hallway. Afterward, some of us met outside to discuss how it went.

One man in our debriefing circle was very upset. His legislator hadn't shown concern for how passionately he felt about the importance of maintaining the program for himself and other people like him. His legislator hadn't seemed to listen to him at all. The program helped him have his daily needs met—the things he couldn't do for himself no matter how much he wished he could. It gave him a chance to live his life outside of an institution. Yet, his elected representative didn't care to hear about it. To this rally participant, it had been a wasted effort.

He had spoken these words with the aid of a talking box attached to his wheelchair. The talking box was operated by his tongue as he moved a small white ball on something which looked like a golf tee to shape letters and words. His tongue touches were translated through his talking box into a computer-generated voice for him. He was unable to hold his head up on his own; it was supported by braces. This man could only move his eyes, his tongue to work his talking box, and his fingers to power his wheelchair.

All I could think of was how big of a deal it had been for him to arrange to come to this rally. For me it had only been a case of grabbing a breakfast bar, filling my bottle of water, jumping into my car, driving to Madison, parking it, and walking a few blocks to the rally location. For him, it had to have involved caregivers helping him dress and eat and get settled in his wheelchair. Then, he needed special transport. All of this would have had to have been arranged in advance. It was incredibly sad to hear him tell us how he felt it had all been a wasted effort—how it was hopeless for him.

Our small circle of people tried to cheer him up the best we could. We tried to help him see he had made an important impression in the rally and at the Capitol—even if his legislator hadn't showed interest.

PERSEVERE BECAUSE YOU GIVE A VOICE TO OTHERS

Sometimes, it *does* take a village. Making changes happen requires us to stick with it—to persevere even in the face of hopelessness or frustration. We continued using our voices as this man did and we achieved our goal of saving the program from elimination. Plus, we achieved so much more in the process! Our network of voices by and for people with disabilities grew significantly and we strengthened our movement in Wisconsin. Should there ever be a reason to stand up for disability rights again, our network is a force to be reckoned with!

This story illustrates another important point: When you feel unheard or disrespected, it doesn't mean you didn't make an important impression. The man at the rally didn't feel his single voice mattered. *Together, we made his voice count.*

LET YOUR IMPACTS FLOW ACROSS THE WORLD

In 2014, I focused my State of the County address entirely on water issues. This address is an annual speech about the status of a county that is delivered by a county executive to her or his community. Afterward, I got tremendous push back from some local legislators, farmers, and an association of growers who wanted to reinvent the facts about water and continue the status quo. I pushed forward on water issues anyway. Around the same time, a very active team of citizens became involved in highlighting groundwater issues. They mobilized others and county groundwater meetings became even more highly attended, regularly overflowing the large rooms in which they were held. This led to creating even more momentum and completing our countywide water quality study in 2017. While I was going to retire in 2018, it didn't mean I wasn't still hoping that positive attention to our water and future would flow beyond my service in public office.

Fast forward over a year since I retired from public office: A citizen stopped me outside the grocery store. He is a groundwater specialist and was a member of the citizen team mentioned above which mobilized many other citizens. He excitedly shared how our groundwater initiatives are indeed flowing forward. He told me he had been hired by a group of citizens in a small village. They wanted his help in getting to the bottom of their water contamination problems. This was a direct follow up from our countywide study which identified water quality issues in their neighborhood. He was working across the whole village to try to help them figure it out and find solutions together. Indeed, the progress continued locally, but there have also been ripples of change across our state, too.

While many places in Wisconsin have been experiencing and studying water problems for years, our high-profile attention on water issues in Portage County reinforced the voices of other citizens in other regions of our state. At last, water quality and providing clean drinking water is now getting "stepped up" consideration statewide!

You never know how far the ripples of your actions might flow. Margaret Mead said, "Never doubt that a small group of thoughtful, committed citizens can change the world. Indeed, it is the only thing that ever has."[62] As an empowered person with this book in hand to help, *you* can be the one who convenes the small group which launches a movement and changes the world. *Imagine that!*

At first, your growth may be undetectable. Your progress might seem insignificant. You might feel like your goal is unattainable. But as you stick with it, you will notice how far you've come and how much you've grown. You will see how small changes are adding up around you. You will feel positive waves of momentum from that progress. Seize every moment. Persevere on your journey. Leave your old self behind for you are becoming someone new.

6

LIVING EMPOWERED: THE NATURE OF YOUR LEGACY

Imagine:

> *Empowered, you stood up for your planet and yourself. It took courage. It required commitment and passion. You had to build your confidence to spread your wings. You stuck with it and your actions have made a positive difference. Ripple effects now flow across your community and beyond. You moved from "me to legacy" when you began living your life dedicated to improving the situation for others and this magnificent planet—when you started living your life **on purpose.** You didn't "settle" for what might come your way, you went out and made it happen. To know the future is brighter, in part, because of your efforts and the changes you have brought about is exceptionally gratifying. And it is all because you chose to leave it better. You, my friend, have become a citizen of this Earth.*

LIVE YOUR LEGACY

In many ways, the nature of our legacy chooses us. It sure did for me. Throughout my life, following my heart gave me momentum. I knew I was here with a purpose on this planet. I just had to figure out what it was and then get on with the business of making this world a better place while applying my highest self to the task. If you haven't already discovered your higher purpose, you will find it when you seek it out. *But where and how, you ask?*

Over time, while I was tapping what I thought were my greatest strengths and learning from my mistakes, I moved closer and closer to discovering what it was. All the while, I gave of my time in service to various people and causes and often stepped outside my comfort zone for a greater good. I figured our community and world deserved the best I could give of me and I wanted to live a life that mattered—not just a routine one, not a boring one, not one to just "make a living." I wanted to *lead* and enjoy a full life.

I tuned in to opportunities around me—ones that naturally came my way—but, also created opportunities by leaping forward even when I hadn't yet gotten my wings. I just had to trust myself to figure it out. Through all these experiences, I homed in on my reason for being here on this planet. It wasn't any kind of a perfect or perfectly happy path for sure. It was a winding path—sometimes a dark one—but I kept searching and following my heart and my talents and being close to Mother Nature to let her guide me and get me through tough times. She repeatedly gave me fresh new dawns when I could begin again or pick up where I left off the day before. These were new 24-hour days—the same days you also get wherever you are. These new dawns gave me a chance to learn more, try even harder or take a different approach. Sometimes, they were new days when I had to forgive myself, kick my own butt, or get back on my feet. There was no such thing as giving up. There was simply too much at stake.

Mother Nature helped me re-center myself when I was knocked off balance. Her lessons taught me how to survive through the rises and falls of life, including how to let go of grief I felt at the loss of loved ones. She reminded me every day of the wonders of living in such an interconnected world—a single blue planet built with a web of life and relationships between all living and nonliving things. When I plugged myself into the power around me, I saw I wasn't alone anymore. I found there was a whole world of people who loved our Earth and our Earth's people as much as me. Her grandeur taught me how "awe" feels and gave me an undying determination to do whatever I could in support of the amazing life and beauty and diversity on this planet.

It will likely be a similar way for you, too. Glimmers of your truest purpose as a human being will be revealed to you, but you will need to be looking for the clues. Then, continuing to follow your heart when you take a stand on issues that matter most to you, more insights will follow. As you step up in passionate service to others and our planet, your purpose will shine through. You will know. Yes, you will know it when you find it—and when it claims you.

Retracing the steps and years of my life, I see now all experiences since I was young were leading me to sharing this moment with you. Getting to the place where my legacy was discovered was one of the greatest "aha" moments of my life. That's when *Empowered: One Planet at a Time* got its wings.

I want the wonders of life on Earth—in natural and human communities—to survive and thrive long after I'm gone. I want you to discover your calling in service to life on Earth so you can enjoy a more vibrant and fulfilling future on this planet. *I am answering my life's call so you can answer your own.*

Living your life *on purpose* will lead you to a life of significance—one that matters beyond yourself. Through this book, you have been equipped with everything you need for creating a significant life and legacy. The next steps are up to you.

PAY IT FORWARD

While I was county executive, we set aside land for a new county park called Steinhaugen. It was 270 acres of land with a great deal of geological, historical, and ecological value. In this age when natural places are often at risk, it was a tremendous opportunity to pay it forward. The landowners who had Steinhaugen in their family for generations wanted to preserve their property "into perpetuity." So did we. Working together, we were able to make it happen when we turned their lands into a county park for silent sports like hiking and cross-country skiing. This became a "forever gift" to future generations. It was a thrill to be part of seeing this project through and knowing we did something together for future generations of people and wildlife.

What about you? What kind of "forever gifts" do you want to give those who come after you? Hopefully by now, you know my intention in offering this book is to help you cultivate the answers to this question in your own heart and mind. Just as hopefully, my dream is that the tools in this book will guide you on your journey so you can be successful and leave the world better for having been here. As you stand up for your planet and yourself, you will unlock your fullest human potential. It happened this way for me. Once you are empowered as a citizen of Planet Earth, you will become aware of a world of possibilities for paying it forward.

START TODAY

Every social or environmental change begins with one person who thinks it should be different and believes they have something to contribute toward improving the situation. Are you that one? Do you want to be able to look back someday and know you gave your "all" to making your world a better place?

Earth Day 1970 became a reality because one person stood up and then thousands of others did, too. These were people who harnessed the power within and around themselves—then stepped up and didn't give up. Their voices—each of their individual voices—couldn't and wouldn't be silenced because they knew their message was too important to go without an appropriate response. The uprising magnified common voices and created a mass wave of change that led to "spasms of rapid-fire lawmaking."[63] Today is a day like that day—a day to start.

> IT IS...OUR NATURE TO CHOOSE LARGE GOALS THAT WHILE DIFFICULT ARE POTENTIALLY GAME-CHANGING AND UNIVERSAL IN BENEFIT. TO STRIVE AGAINST ODDS ON BEHALF OF ALL OF LIFE WOULD BE HUMANITY AT ITS MOST NOBLE.
> –E. O. WILSON[64]

What we do in our lives—the choices we make, the actions we take—leave this world forever different. It is up to us to decide what kind of difference we want to make.[65] Like the Monarch caterpillar giving its "all" to form its chrysalis on its journey to realizing its fullest potential when it takes flight as a magnificent migratory butterfly, so it can be for us. When we give our all, we unleash our fullest potential. What a glorious way to go about living!

Throughout this book, I've been advocating for you to write down some thoughts as you are going through your journey so you can capture turning points and reflect on your growth. Journaling may also give you glimpses of your own future and legacy. I thought sharing an excerpt from what I wrote in my journal in March 2019 on the eve of beginning to write this book could help illustrate this magic as I have strived to live my legacy.

March 13, 2019

I've been making some progress and now have the job of outlining the book—the overview, the chapters, the flow and sense of that. I've been stumbling on this. Thinking too hard, I thought I would write to my own "stuck self" like Kary Oberbrunner[66] puts it, to tell the story and hopefully break through. So, I sit in bed, pen in hand, dog next to me, and a cup of coffee within reach…

Dear Stuck Self? Remember when you were young and dreamed of being called a "naturalist" one day but there was a huge challenge ahead because the world seemed limitless with natural wonder (HOW RIGHT I WAS) and you/I learned I couldn't know it all? Remember my secret place behind the cabin where I would go and explore? It was out of view of others though I was close enough to keep the cabin in view. The soil was sandy and there were lichens growing there. I would sit quietly. Dream. Explore. Feel wind beneath this little girl's dream-wings….

That's when Dad was our guide to the outdoors—whether we were camping or just in the backyard or garden—he was a store of nature knowledge. He was comfortable in his "outdoor skin" and taught me to be the same. I wish that for everyone.

Stuck Self, I remember so many more walks and gardens as Tom and I lived in other places around the world. I remember when I dreamed of "environmental education" as it was just then being developed and going on to earn my master's degree. At first, it seemed so far away and impossible.

My journey continued: Having one-to-one time with the Father of Earth Day. Earth Day 1990. German-American Earth Days. Hungary. The whole wide world became my home—people everywhere, all different cultures and communities. It all opened up for me.

Meeting the Girl Guides from behind the Iron Curtain had a huge impact on me because it showed me how we can be imprisoned in unthinkable ways—especially when our voices are shut down and we are deprived of the freedom of association with our fellow human beings. They were only wanting to make the world a better place!

In my own process of learning to step up, I remember being upset in Alaska when I called in an abandoned car to the county. It had gallons (I think five or six) of black oil in the backseat. Someone had been doing target practice on the old car, but the containers of black oil were still intact. The county worker on the phone said, "Well, what do you want me to do? I've got over 200 abandoned cars in the county." And all I could think of was one drop of oil could contaminate many gallons of drinking water—and this person didn't care....

There were other times when I stood up on social and environmental issues, too. On sexual harassment, for example. On mistreatment of a family member in our health care system and many more times. I became braver and more willing to trust myself to find my way through—to keep marching. Remember that deep courage? Remember the difficulties from time to time, but also the rewards of leap years of growth as I persevered through the toughest times? How I always sought lessons and healing from nature?

I remember my "Caring for the Earth" keynote in Sonthofen, Germany, at the international conference when I was pregnant with April just a week before she died. What power there was in the closing presentation! I had illustrated the music of "From a Distance"[67] with slides from the Iraq war. There were contrasting images of nature, youth, and love. Tears were everywhere among hundreds of people in attendance. I saw then how caring for and about nature could be a tool for peace and hope in the world. A world that God or Mother Nature or whatever higher power we believe in is watching. And that really set the stage for Empowered: One Planet at a Time. I can see it clearly now: Every experience had been a steppingstone which led me in this direction to this capstone of my life....

We can't always predict what next ripples will happen beyond our time—but knowing we "gave our all" <u>during</u> our time is satisfying. It leaves us with no regrets. Each one of us would love to have "take backs" but we don't get that chance. We can only learn and lean forward. So, taking charge of my life is perhaps the bravest thing I've ever done...

My whole life has prepared me for this. So, "Stuck Self," you've found yourself pushing through, creating a life journey made from love for nature and people—particularly younger people. You have dedicated your life to helping others develop stronger connections and passions. Sharing enthusiasm and energy, you have stuck your neck out for yourself—your own goals—but also for other people and for what's right on this planet. Your values are strong. You have a sense of uncompromising on the basics of healthy rights to air, water, and balanced ecological systems. You have been part of some projects "into perpetuity" which is humbling—because this is the taste of legacy that matters. Your children are and always have been "children of the world."

There's a way to put it all together and that way will become this book and the related journey of sharing the story so others can feel wind beneath their wings. So they can feel part of a flock, so they can feel hopeful and ready and courageous and capable and committed....and empowered to help save this loveliest of blue planets.

WE CAN DREAM THE WORLD DIFFERENTLY.
–TERRY TEMPEST WILLIAMS[68]

It seems overwhelming. It may seem like it's too late. Or not enough people care. Or what I can do is a little splash in a big sea, but perhaps the greatest gift of all is that we can break it down and take it one planet at a time. To stand up is to believe in ourselves.

To define what matters to us. And not to wait for others but to ask them to join us. Not to defer. But to start now. To understand that no matter what, no matter where I live, no matter what my own situation, I AM A CITIZEN OF PLANET EARTH and together we, empowered citizens of this planet, can turn the tide. We can take back our rights to the freedoms of clean air and water. We can reconnect with our natural world where love and life grow and develop environmental ethics in our children. We have a voice—millions of them—and the power of those voices and votes can far outweigh special interests which selfishly want to have their way and wealth at the expense of our children and our health and our future.

This is a long game—not a flash in the pan. On the way to feeling empowered, we have to overcome our own demons—like "I am not enough," "I don't know enough," or "My actions won't matter." We also have to move beyond "I'll be in danger" or "I'll be seen as _____ or hated for _____." We can't worry that we may not be able to finish the job, either. We just have to start. We must stand up for what we know to be right. We must find a way—then persevere. There is always something we can contribute.

All the technology in the world will not substitute for thinking, caring people who are done letting their planet be destroyed. This web of life is yours and mine. It's our lifeblood. Start where you are. Gather friends. Seek power in numbers. This is about justice. Peace. Transformation. Living in harmony. Taking it one step, one planet at a time.

It's time to lift off on your own journey. Trust your internal compass for direction. Believe in yourself and all you can become on and for this Earth. Follow your heart and your talents in service to other people and our planet and you are on your way to living a meaningful, significant and exciting life. Don't be afraid to shake it up or step out in front when others may not. They may need you to be courageous for them. Don't shy away from standing tall on your values. What else are they for? Show others the way. Teach them. Lead them. Lift them up. Live your life empowered in every dimension.

TAKE IT ONE PLANET AT A TIME

Whether you dream of (or already have) a career in business, education, human services, law, research, government, agriculture, engineering, art, healthcare, or some other amazing field, the Earth needs you to stand up and be part of transforming the ways we work and live.

Our Earth desperately needs people like you who proudly and confidently stand up and shine in your moment as a leader who says "enough is enough" when it is time to say that and "let's figure this out together" when it makes sense to start organizing for change. Our planet needs the voices of empowered people—a mass movement of them like you—to forge a new way forward. Our times call for young adults like you who are our leaders of the future to bravely step up now and take back their destiny on this Earth. We are headed in directions on this planet which are exceptionally concerning, and it will take the actions of multitudes who vote, who speak out, who form coalitions, who bridge divides and who ultimately help us conquer the social, political, cultural, and environmental challenges facing us.

Your future is calling. Listen for it. Imagine it. Live up to it. Become it. Yes, you can. Just take it one planet at a time.

I have faith in you.

AFTERWORD BY DIETER BÖHN, BERND SCHMITT, AND HELMER VOGEL WITH PATTY DREIER

Together, One Planet at a Time

As co-founders of German-American Earth Day and lifelong collaborators on environmental education projects, we hope you will be as lucky as we have been! We have found one of the greatest gifts of living empowered is the way it has opened up the whole world to us—a world of wonderful people and extraordinary possibilities. We speak from experience. Across the Earth, we have taken it one planet at a time together since we met twenty-eight years ago!

None of us can remember exactly how we met. It seems like we have known each other for our whole lives. That's the beauty of it. We have always been "us." Though Germany and the United States are far apart on a map, we are close together in our hearts and visions for Planet Earth.

The outcomes of our German-American partnership have been more amazing than we ever dreamed possible when we first came together. Why? Because we were positive about finding a way forward *together* rather than expecting things *not* to work when it seemed too difficult to cross language, political, and cultural barriers. Even when we had just begun helping military families in Würzburg learn to sort their waste in accordance with German law, no one pointed fingers. We just asked how we could help each other and sought a common understanding.

We also sought opportunities to make more lasting impacts—like our annual tradition of German-American Earth Day which went on for fifteen years until the American military drawdown in Germany. Or, when we created models like the *Umweltstation Würzburg* (Environmental Station) located downtown in the City of Würzburg where people of all ages, backgrounds, and nations connect, learn, and grow. The *Umweltstation* model has been recognized by leaders in Germany and other European countries. There are now sixty of these learning stations located across Europe where many thousands of citizens of many nations come together to participate in programs that reinforce a message about sharing a single planet.

As you set out to stand up for your planet and yourself, we hope you will follow in our footsteps: Seek common understandings and focus on ways to make lasting impacts. We believe that these approaches will help you achieve the same kinds of successes we have experienced. As our models have demonstrated, waves of change will follow—and that is just what our planet needs.

In many ways, sharing an international partnership seems to have expanded our world—our thinking, our exposure to new experiences, and our resources like the Goethe Institute which funded one of our collaborations to fly Patty from Alaska to Germany. It has also given us additional networks and strengths to tap when we needed them—even half-way around the world. Our international partnership has also magnified the fun! We have shared university program exchanges, field trips, conferences, task groups, delegations, family visits, and toasts of our favorite beverages to our lifelong friendships.

Interestingly, our international partnership has also helped to shrink our world because it has reinforced the fact that we are one—a single community of people on this planet. Even across the miles, we depend on each other to be pulling in the same direction to protect our children's future.

We are family. We want you to join us in seeing our planet as one world. It is one world upon which all of us depend—together. We all breathe the same air, drink the same water, and depend on the same biosphere to live. But it is also one world of exceptional wisdom and hope for the future. We encourage you to reach out to others across the planet to build coalitions. Like it did for us, we want you to experience how it enhances your perspective, unleashes new potential, and boosts optimism as you face global challenges head on.

We know many of our environmental and social problems are not easily solved. We point out that in the history of mankind, there were often dark periods of great challenge. *And people overcame them by coming together.* It can be this way for us now—with your help.

A new *Umweltstation Würzburg* opened in 2019. Its green building design is now part of its model to teach generations as they come to learn, to be empowered and to work for a brighter future. Seek out these kinds of local education centers to connect and grow. They will help you find your way. It is *our* world to be sure—*but it is your future.*

We believe it is possible to overcome the challenges facing us now on Earth, but we must act without delay! We must embrace the opportunities. Learn. Seek partners across our communities and the globe. Stand up with courage and confidence. Highlight problems—but always become part of solutions. Let experiences in nature teach and inspire and remind us what an amazing world this is and why we should never give up.

We ask you to keep in mind there are millions—even billions—of people who simply do not have the time to care about their environment because they are struggling to live and care for their children. If you are reading this book, then you have a chance to apply yourself in ways others may never be able to locally or across our planet. Please. *This is a glorious home—Planet Earth.* She needs you. We all do.

Professor Emeritus Dr. Dieter Böhn, Department of Geography, University of Würzburg, Research Emphasis on Educating for Sustainability with Partners in the U.S. and China

Dr. Bernd M. Schmitt, Retired in 2018 from the City of Würzburg—European Union Funding Forum—Department of Economics, Science and Marketing

Dr. Helmer Vogel, Diplom-Geographer, Former Academic Director of Didactics of Geography, Department of Geography and Geology, University of Würzburg. Currently, Consulting on Sustainable Tourism and Vocational Education in Tourism in Europe, Africa and Asia

Patty Dreier, Author of *Empowered: One Planet at a Time*; Founder and CEO, Blue Spring Innovations, LLC, Stevens Point, Wisconsin

APPENDICES

WITH THIS TREE

© 1991 Patty Dreier

FOR MOTHER (*FÜR MUTTER*)

English verse: Patty Dreier, 1988
German verse: Helmer Vogel, 1991

© 1988 Patty Dreier

*Note: Guitar chords are in a different key.

English translation of German verse

For Mother

I sing this song to you, my Mother,
for that what I here have,
for the wonderful living,
for peace, love, every day.
And when all of the people of the Earth
care more about you,
You'll have not so much to care about me.

THE FIRST GERMAN-AMERICAN EARTH DAY 1991 AND GIANT EARTH PUZZLE

AN EXAMPLE OF "MODELING THE CHANGE" AND "EDUCATING PEOPLE IN SUPPORT OF CHANGE"

Before the German-American Earth Day event to be held at the American school at Leighton Barracks in Würzburg in April 1991, we planned three pre-activities for German and American teachers to use in their respective third grade classrooms to prepare their students for the event.

The first activity involved learning to sing *For Mother* in both English and German. (A copy of this song is provided in the Appendices.) This song which had been sung a year before for Earth Day 1990 in San Antonio, Texas, was now translated into German.

The second pre-activity for school classes was to have each child paint a wooden puzzle piece for a giant 150-piece Earth Puzzle we had designed for them. The puzzle showed a map outlining the continents and larger islands of the world with the Atlantic Ocean in the middle to center on the geographic relationship between the United States and Germany. The children did not know where their puzzle piece fit—only that if it had a *W* on it, the code represented *water* (or <u>*wasser*</u> in German) and the palette of colors they could use to paint areas on their puzzle piece with that code included blue, purple, or white. If their piece of the puzzle had an *L* on it, the code represented *land* (the same word in both English and German though pronounced differently in the two languages). The palette of colors to be used for pieces of the puzzle with the *L* code included green, red, yellow, orange, or brown.

We made sure to mix the pieces across the German and American school classes so there would be optimal mixing of children at the event when it came to assembling the puzzle. We thought a puzzle would act as an international language because most children knew how to put jigsaw puzzles together without special instruction. A puzzle would get them working cooperatively toward a common solution.

The third pre-activity involved each student "adopting" an endangered animal. Each child chose and learned about "their" animal—including where its natural habitat on Earth was located. They also drew and cut out a picture of their animal.

On the day of the event, each student walked in the door with a large colorful puzzle piece under their arm and the picture they drew of their adopted animal. After a welcome in both languages from our German-American leadership team, the children began to assemble the puzzle. To make solving the puzzle easier to accomplish during our program timeframe, we had written a number on the back of each piece representing a *zone* (the same word in both languages though pronounced differently). We asked the children with *Zone 1* written on the back of their puzzle piece to sit on the floor in one area. We asked the students with *Zone 2* on their pieces to sit together, and so on. Each zone had ten puzzle pieces. The children assembled their zone of the puzzle and then slid the fifteen sections together to finish assembling the giant puzzle on the gymnasium floor. It was incredibly exciting to see them freely interacting with each other as they cooperated to unveil the co-created masterpiece.

After the giant Earth Puzzle was assembled, German and American officials spoke to the group. The U.S. Army Colonel held an Earth Ball as he spoke about each of us sharing the same planet. That image was captured in a timeless photo by local media, including a military newspaper that was distributed to Americans living across the area. The Lord Mayor of Würzburg also addressed the children. German and American dignitaries participated in the whole event together demonstrating they were united as leaders in the community. The song, *For Mother,* was sung in both languages.

For some children, this was their first time to interact with children from another country. We believed we had begun to break down barriers when we showed them how they were more alike than different. One child had stayed home from school that day because he was ill. His teacher forgot to bring his puzzle piece along. This resulted in the assembled puzzle missing one piece including New Zealand. Another child had adopted the endangered Kiwi (*Apteryx sp.*), a flightless bird native to New Zealand. When each student was instructed to put the picture of his or her adopted animal in the place of its native home on the Earth Puzzle, the child with the Kiwi became sad. New Zealand was missing from the puzzle. It was as if Planet Earth no longer had a place for his endangered animal. This was a powerful teachable moment—and we used it!

—◦—

Long after I left Germany, German-American Earth Day continued to bring children and community leaders together. In preparation for this book, I surveyed my German colleagues, Dieter, Bernd, and Charly about our collaborations. I asked them what they believed was the most important work we accomplished together. Resoundingly, each of them answered *German-American Earth Day and the ways it brought our nations, our leaders—and us—together through the years.*

ENDNOTES

1. The Nelson Institute. (2019). The Nelson legacy. *Nelson Institute for Environmental Studies, University of Wisconsin-Madison.* Retrieved on August 2, 2019, from https://www.nelson.wisc.edu/about/nelson-legacy.php

2. Maranuss, D. (1999). *When Pride Still Mattered: A Life of Vince Lombardi.* New York, NY: Simon and Schuster.

3. The Nelson Institute. (n.d.). Introduction: The Earth Day story and Gaylord Nelson. *The Nelson Institute for Environmental Studies, University of Wisconsin-Madison.* Retrieved on August 2, 2019, from http://www.nelsonearthday.net/earth-day/index.php

4. Rome, A. (2013). *The genius of Earth Day: How a 1970 teach-in unexpectedly made the first green generation* (p. 59). New York, NY: Hill and Wang.

5. The Nelson Institute. (n.d.). The living tradition of Earth Day. *The Nelson Institute, University of Wisconsin-Madison.* Retrieved on August 2, 2019, from http://www.nelsonearthday.net/earth-day/living-tradition.php

6. Earth Day Network in Association with American Experience. (n.d.). The environmental decade: Impacts and legislation. *WETA Public Television and Classical Music for Greater Washington.* Retrieved August 2, 2019, from https://weta.org/files/2Legislation_Lesson%20Planw_chapters.pdf

7. Wisconsin Department of Natural Resources. (2017). Nitrate in drinking water. *Wisconsin Department of Natural Resources.* Retrieved August 2, 2019, from https://dnr.wi.gov/files/pdf/pubs/dg/dg0001.pdf

8. McCasland, M., Trautmann, N. M., Porter, K. S., & Wagenet, R. J. (2012). Nitrate: Health effects in drinking water. *Cornell University Pesticide Safety Education Program.* Retrieved August 2, 2019, from http://psep.cce.cornell.edu/facts-slides-self/facts/nit-heef-grw85.aspx

9. Wisconsin Department of Natural Resources. (2017). Nitrate in drinking water. *Wisconsin Department of Natural Resources.* Retrieved August 2, 2019, from https://dnr.wi.gov/files/pdf/pubs/dg/dg0001.pdf

10. Todd, B. (2019, January 26). Nitrates: The canary in the coal mine and other concerns. *Agrinews.* Retrieved August 2, 2019, from https://www.postbulletin.com/agrinews/news/minnesota/nitrates-the-canary-in-the-coal-mine-and-other-concerns/article_81896a6c-233d-11e9-9633-6b39a22cbfe6.html

11. Engleson, D. C. (1985, p. 4). *A guide to curriculum planning in environmental education.* Madison, WI: Wisconsin Department of Public Instruction.

12. Díaz, S., Settele, J., Brondízio, E., Ngo, H. T., Guèze, M., Agard, J. . . . Zayas, C. (2019, May 6). Summary for policymakers of the global assessment report on biodiversity and ecosystem services of the intergovernmental science-policy platform on bio-diversity and ecosystem services. *Intergovernmental Science-Policy Platform on Biodiversity and Ecosystem Services.* Retrieved on August 2, 2019, from https://www.ipbes.net/sites/default/files/downloads/spm_unedited_advance_for_posting_htn.pdf

13. Djoghlaf, A. (2007, May 22). Message on the occasion of the international day for biological diversity. United Nations Environment Programme. Retrieved July 31, 2019, from https://www.cbd.int/doc/speech/2007/sp-2007-05-22-es-en.pdf

14. World Population Balance. (2010-2019). *World Population Balance Family of Sites.* Retrieved July 31, 2019, from https://www.worldpopulationbalance.org/faq

15. Worldometers. (2019). *Worldometers Family of Sites.* Retrieved July 22, 2019, from https://www.worldometers.info/world-population/

16. Global Climate Dashboard. (n.d.). *National Oceanic Atmospheric Administration Climate.gov Family of Sites.* Retrieved July 23, 2019, from https://www.climate.gov/

17. To see a photo of trail sign with Gaylord Nelson's quote on it, go to https://www.bluespring.net

18. Curie, M. (n.d.). *AZQuotes.com.* Retrieved July 31, 2019, from https://www.azquotes.com/quote/69291

19. London, J. (2015). *Jack London on Adventure: Words of Wisdom from an Expert Adventurer* (p. 10). New

York, NY: Skyhorse Publishing, Inc. on *AZQuotes. com*. Retrieved July 30, 2019, from https://www. azquotes.com/author/9002-Jack_London

20. Mind mapping. (2019). *Mindmapping.com*. Retrieved on August 30, 2019, from https://www. mindmapping.com/

21. Wilson, E. O. (1984). *Biophilia*. Cambridge, MA: Harvard University Press.

22. Kaplan, R., & Kaplan, S. (1989). *The experience of nature: A psychological perspective* (pp. 195-197). Cambridge, NY: Cambridge University Press.

23. Coles, J. (2016, April 20). How nature is good for our health and happiness. [Weblog for *BBC Earth*]. Retrieved July 23, 2019, from http://www. bbc.com/earth/story/20160420-how-nature-is-go od-for-our-health-and-happiness

24. Kuo, M. (2015). How might contact with nature promote human health? Promising mechanisms and a possible central pathway. *Frontiers in Psychology*, 6:1093. Retrieved July 21, 2019, from https://www.frontiersin.org/articles/10.3389/ fpsyg.2015.01093/full

25. American Public Health Association. (2013, November 5). Improving health and wellness through access to nature. *American Public Health Association Public Policy 20137*. Retrieved July 21, 2019, from https:// www.apha.org/policies-and-advocacy/ public-health-policy-statements/ policy-database/2014/07/08/09/18/ improving-health-and-wellness-through-acces s-to-nature

26. Li, Q. (2018). *Forest bathing: how trees can help you find health and happiness.* New York, NY: Viking.

27. Muir, J. (1918). *Steep Trails California – Utah – Nevada – Washington – Oregon – The Grand Canyon* (Chapter 9 Mormon Lilies). Retrieved July 29, 2019, from https://vault.sierraclub.org/john_muir_exhibit/writings/steep_trails/chapter_9.aspx

28. Emerson, R. W. (1836). *Nature.* Retrieved July 29, 2019, from https://www.cliffsnotes.com/literature/t/thoreau-emerson-and-transcendentalism/emersons-nature/major-themes

29. Burroughs, J. (1912). *Time and Change* (p. 244). New York, NY: Wm. H. Wise & Company.

30. Angelou, M. [Maya]. (2011, October 25). Facebook post retrieved July 31, 2019, from https://www.facebook.com/MayaAngelou/posts/10150373232074796

31. Davis, M. (2017, September 14). *Every Day Spirit: A Daybook of Wisdom, Joy and Peace.* Florida: Rich River Publishing Company.

32. Aurelius, M. (n.d.). *Goodreads.com.* Retrieved July 31, 2019, from https://www.goodreads.com/quotes/21296-dwell-on-the-beauty-of-life-watch-the-stars-and

33. Frank, A. (1991). *The diary of a young girl: The definitive edition* (p. 194). Frank, O. H. & Pressler, M. (Eds.). New York, NY: Bantam Books.

34. Smith, H. (n.d.). *AZQuotes.com.* Retrieved July 31, 2019, from https://www.azquotes.com/quote/1360158

35. John Burroughs Association. (2013-2015). *John Burroughs Association Family of Sites.* Retrieved July 26, 2019, from http://www.johnburroughsassociation.org/

36. New World Encyclopedia. (2016, August 18). Iron curtain. Retrieved July 31, 2019, from http://www.newworldencyclopedia.org/entry/Iron_curtain

37. Winston, G. (2014, May 23). *War History Online.* Retrieved July 31, 2019, from https://www.warhistoryonline.com/war-articles/start-end-iron-curtain.html

38. Kennedy, C., & Dreier, P. (1990). *Earth Matters: A Challenge for Environmental Action.* New York, NY: Girl Scouts of the USA.

39. Roosevelt, T. (n.d.). *AZQuotes.com.* Retrieved July 30, 2019, from https://www.azquotes.com/quote/250956

40. Izaak Walton League of America. (n.d.). Join the clean water challenge. *Izaak Walton League of America.* Retrieved July 26, 2019, from https://www.iwla.org/conservation/water/clean-water-challenge

41. Journey North. (1997 – 2019). Report sightings of specific species. *Journey North Family of Sites.* Retrieved June 23, 2019, from www.journeynorth.org

42. The Cornell Lab of Ornithology. (n.d.). eBird to report bird sightings. *The Cornell Lab of Ornithology Family of Sites.* Retrieved June 23, 2019, from https://ebird.org/home

43. National Geographic. (1996 – 2019). Citizen science. *National Geographic Family of Sites.* Retrieved

July 31, 2019, from https://www.nationalgeographic.org/idea/citizen-science-projects/

44. National Audubon Society. (n.d.). Christmas bird count and other citizen science opportunities. *National Audubon Society Family of Sites.* Retrieved June 23, 2019, from www.nationalaudubon.org

45. New York Botanical Garden. (n.d.). NYBG citizen science. *New York Botanical Garden Family of Sites.* Retrieved July 30, 2019, from https://www.nybg.org/plant-research-and-conservation/center-for-conservation-strategy/citizen-science/

46. California Academy of Sciences & National Geographic Society. (n.d.). iNaturalist. *iNaturalist.org Family of Sites.* Retrieved August 19, 2019, from https://www.inaturalist.org/

47. Wilson, W. (1913). Wilson's wise words. *Bob Chapman's Truly Human Leadership.* Retrieved on July 31, 2019, from https://www.trulyhumanleadership.com/?p=259

48. Ghandi, M. (n.d.). We must live the changes we want to see in the world. *Quote Investigator.* Retrieved July 31, 2019, from https://quoteinvestigator.com/2017/10/23/be-change/

49. Hayden, A. (2019, January 28). Ecological footprint. *Encyclopaedia Britannica.* Retrieved July 28, 2019, from https://www.britannica.com/science/ecological-footprint

50. Ecological Footprint. (2003 – 2019). *Global Footprint Network Family of Sites.* Retrieved July 28, 2019, from https://www.footprintnetwork.org/

51. Fuller, R. B. (n.d.). *AZQuotes.com.* Retrieved July 31, 2019, from https://www.azquotes.com/author/5231-R_Buckminster_Fuller

52. Peracchio, T. (2017, July 6). How many times did Thomas Alva Edison fail exactly? *Quora.* Retrieved July 31, 2019, from https://www.quora.com/How-many-times-did-Thomas-Alva-Edison-fail-exactly

53. Sieg, K. (2019, June 12). Sustainable lifestyles: Progress, not perfection! Community presentation from Recycling Connections, IDEA Center of CREATE Portage County, Stevens Point, Wisconsin.

54. Lennon, J. (n.d.). *AZQuotes.com.* Retrieved August 1, 2019, from https://www.azquotes.com/author/8717-John_Lennon

55. Peale, N. V. (1970). *Norman Vincent Peale's treasury of courage and confidence. AZQuotes.com.* Retrieved August 1, 2019, from https://www.azquotes.com/quote/227551

56. Cather, W. (1927). *Death comes to the archbishop* (Book 2). *AZQuotes.com.* Retrieved July 31, 2019, from https://www.azquotes.com/quote/51087

57. Highland, C. (2004). *Meditations of Ralph Waldo Emerson: Into the green future* (p. 125). Berkeley, CA: Wilderness Press.

58. Laozi. (n.d.). *AZQuotes.com.* Retrieved August 1, 2019, from https://www.azquotes.com/author/19615-Laozi

59. Eisley, L. (1969). The star thrower. *The unexpected universe* (p. 67). Orlando, FL: Harcourt Brace & Company.

60. Centers for Disease Control Division for Heart Disease and Stroke Prevention. (n. d.). *Evaluation guide: Developing and using a logic model.* U.S. Department of Health and Human Services. Retrieved September 5, 2019, from https://www.cdc.gov/dhdsp/docs/logic_model.pdf

61. IRIS is an acronym for Include, Respect, I Self-Direct. Wisconsin Department of Health Services. Retrieved August 2, 2019, from https://www.dhs.wisconsin.gov/iris/index.htm

62. Mead, M., & Textor, R. (2005). *The world ahead: An anthropologist anticipates the future* (p. 12). Oxford, NY: Berghahn Books.

63. Klein, N. (2014, p. 461). *This changes everything: Capitalism vs the climate.* New York, NY: Simon & Schuster Paperbacks.

64. Wilson, E. O. (2019, September 6). Half-Earth Day 2019. *E.O. Wilson Biodiversity Foundation.* Retrieved on September 8, 2019, from https://www.half-earthproject.org/half-earth-day-2019/

65. Goodall, J. (2017). *AZQuotes.com.* Retrieved August 14, 2019, from https://www.azquotes.com/author/5682-Jane_Goodall/tag/making-a-difference

66. Oberbrunner, K. (2019). Who module video (0:45). *Author Academy Elite.* Retrieved March 1, 2019, from https://authoracademyelite.com/member-home/whomodule

67. Vezner, J., & Longacre, S. (1991). From a distance. Sung by Kathy Matthea on *Time passes by* [Recorded by Mercury Records a Division of UMG Recordings, Inc.]. Retrieved on September 9, 2019, from https://video.search.yahoo.com/

search/video?fr=mcafee&p=From+a+Distance+mu-sic+with+Kathy+Matthea#id=2&vid=ef9eae-42181b5a697205618d41fe500c&action=click

68. Williams, T. T. (2015). Preface. In T. Berry, *The dream of the earth* (p. v.). Berkeley, CA: Counterpoint.

DISCUSSION QUESTIONS FOR READING GROUPS

FOREWORD

1. Discuss what you think about Aberdeen Leary's essay, "We Cannot Be Too Loud."

CHAPTER 1

2. Reflect on the title and subtitle of Chapter 1. What first comes to mind when you consider "your Earth, your present, your future?"

3. Why do you believe the author wrote "your future begins with you?" In what ways do you live with your future in mind?

4. Suppose you were asked to chauffeur the Father of Earth Day and had one-to-one time with him like the author did. What would you have said to him?

5. Discuss Gaylord Nelson's response to the author's gratitude about being the founder of Earth Day. Do you agree with the credit he gave to others? Why or why not?

6. If you could have one-to-one time with anyone (alive or dead) to talk about environmental or social

issues, who would it be and why? What would you ask/discuss with that person?

7. What do you think or how do you feel when people say, "It's not my problem?"

8. How do you feel about the author's point about it being your business to stand up on issues beyond your community and your country's borders?

9. Give an example of how standing up for your planet is the same thing as standing up for yourself.

CHAPTER 2

10. What do you care about so deeply you are willing to stand up for it?

11. What roles do you believe courage and confidence play in addressing issues of concern? What would happen if you had one and significantly lacked the other?

12. What would you have done if the door-pounding, bullying situation had happened to you?

13. What did you learn about yourself from the "Tracing Your Roots" exercise?

14. What are your pivot points of courage? Why?

15. What platforms for action have begun to take shape in your life?

16. What are your roots to the land or your community and how do these roots give you a unique perspective?

17. What do you think about the author's statement, "When you own it deep inside, you will discover the power within you."

18. How have your values been tested in your life?

19. If you knew you could absolutely make a significant difference, for what would you stand up fearlessly?

20. The author mentioned "the wondrous powers of nature." What do you believe they are?

21. How have you tapped nature-health connections in your own life? What connections are you most curious about and why?

22. How do you think getting people to see themselves as having closer connections with nature can help us solve environmental problems? Is it equally important for urban and rural dwellers? Why or why not?

23. The author provided nature quotes. Which of the quotes resonate the most with you and why? Find and share other quotes. Why do they resonate with you?

24. Share some passages you find interesting in the nature literature of John Burroughs, Aldo Leopold, John Muir, Sigurd Olson, Henry David Thoreau or another author of your choosing. Why do you find the passages interesting?

25. The author referred to "zoom out" and "zoom in" experiences. Can you think of other activities which fit into each of these categories to expand personal connections with nature?

26. Participate in "zoom out" and "zoom in" activities and tell stories about your experiences.

27. Do you believe both "zoom out" and "zoom in" experiences are important in tapping the powers of nature? Why or why not?

28. Discuss the author's poem, "With a Monarch's Grace." What lines resonate the most with you and why?

29. What experiences have you had which have given you a sense of awe about your world? How have those experiences affected you? Some say that experiencing a sense of awe is important in helping people develop a sense of purpose in life. What do you think?

30. What do you think about the quote from Huston Smith, "The larger the island of knowledge, the longer the shoreline of wonder" referenced in this chapter?

31. The author wrote, "Nature literally grounds us. It sustains us. It is who we are. What we discover in nature is ourselves." What do you believe she meant by these words?

CHAPTER 3

32. Discuss the Iron Curtain story. What is the key take-away for you?

33. Discuss your key take-aways from the Earth Day 1990 story about Hands-On Earth Peace.

34. Discuss ways you have maximized power around you in a past situation and what it meant to the outcome in that situation.

35. Discuss an experience when you did not maximize the power around you. What did that experience teach you? If you had a "do-over" what would you do differently and why?

CHAPTER 4

36. Review the *Individual Readiness* and *Group Readiness Checklists*. Why do you believe the author recommended "agree" or "strongly agree" for all the items on the list prior to action?

37. What could happen if you act before you are ready on specific items noted on the *Individual Readiness* and *Group Readiness Checklists*? Can you think of examples in your own life, school/university, or community when there was action taken before complete readiness? How might the outcome have been different if readiness for action had been improved?

38. Identify current examples of local and/or global issues being addressed by other individuals/groups who are concerned about them. What methods for action are being used? How effective do you believe they are? Why do you think so?

39. Brainstorm examples of SMILES methods of action that could be used to address a specific, real-life local or global issue of concern to you/your group. How would you decide which one might be most effective as your first action toward a solution?

40. Which SMILES methods for action would you be (or are you) most comfortable with and why? Which ones would you be (or are you) least comfortable with and why? What do you think it would take for you to use a SMILES action method you are less comfortable with using?

41. Discuss the quote by Woodrow Wilson.

42. Discuss the author's statement, "When you are eligible to vote and do not show up to vote, you give your power away."

43. Discuss why you think the author recommended constructive ways to move forward as opposed to demeaning those who have differing views.

44. What role do you think "conflict" plays in finding solutions to environmental or social problems?

45. Why is it a valuable strategy to equip others so they can take action?

46. Thinking about a local issue for which "Educating People in Support of Change" could be used as an action strategy, discuss ways you might assess knowledge and skills gaps of the target audience. Which assessment would you prefer to use and why?

47. Discuss your main take-aways from the solid waste management story that led to the first German-American Earth Day.

CHAPTER 5

48. Why is it important to sustain yourself when you stand up on environmental and social issues? What approaches do you currently take to sustain yourself when you must persevere? The author provided some suggestions for coping and persevering. What new approaches would you consider trying in the future?

49. Have you ever "run out" of endurance for a challenge in your life? What happened? What would you do differently if you had a "do-over?"

50. Some say that a key to the movement for greater sustainability on Earth is for each of us to live more lightly on the planet. What do you think? Discuss how a sustainability movement might also be considered a movement *within* people.

51. Discuss how do you feel about the author's statement, "There is no such thing as failing when you approach your issue with a heart for serving people and our planet." Make a case for the author being right or being wrong about this.

52. Why do you believe the author advocates for celebrating gains?

53. Think about a challenge or goal in your own life. Share gains—even small ones—you have made in addressing that challenge or goal.

54. How do you believe your journey through life so far has changed you? Have you experienced any "personal transformations?" Share if you feel comfortable doing so.

55. Describe situations in your life which illustrate the author's statement, "As you seek to change the world, you become changed."

56. What role do you think "reflection" plays in seeking to grow from life experiences? What tools for reflection do you use in your life right now? The author advocates for journaling as a useful tool for reflection. What do you think?

57. Watch a video of a butterfly going through complete metamorphosis. Discuss the lessons it teaches you about your planet. What insights does it give you about yourself?

58. Discuss the author's statement, "When we live life as empowered people, we are never the same again."

59. In what ways do you think standing up for your planet and yourself will change you or in what ways has it already changed you?

60. When the author wrote, "Tough times are those times when some of our greatest life lessons are nearest at hand," what do you think she meant? Do you have any examples in your life of this being the case? Share if you feel comfortable doing so.

61. Share examples from your life that illustrate the author's point, "When you feel unheard or disrespected, it doesn't mean you didn't make an important impression."

62. Discuss the idea, "At first, your growth may seem undetectable." How has this been proven to be true in your life?

CHAPTER 6

63. What legacies have been left for you by those who came before you? How do those legacies make you feel?

64. Have you ever before given thought to creating a legacy of your own to pass on to others?

65. Discuss the author's statement, "in many ways, the nature of our legacy chooses us." Do you agree? Why or why not?

66. The author mentions that she thinks you have a higher purpose. What do you think? Why does "purpose" matter?

67. How do you believe someone can go about discovering their higher purpose if they don't feel that they know what it is right now?

68. What does it look like when someone *lives life on purpose*? Do you? What difference do you think it makes?

69. Have you ever encountered your Stuck Self? How did you overcome it?

70. Describe what you believe are the characteristics of an "agent for change." Which of these characteristics do you have now? Which ones do you aspire to develop within yourself?

71. What is your advice for someone who expresses they are "a little splash in a big sea" which makes them feel hopeless in bringing about change?

72. Have you ever thought of yourself as a "Citizen of Planet Earth" before? If so, when? If not, why not?

73. Of what value is it if people see themselves as citizens of the whole planet? What do you think it would take to engage more people in seeing themselves this way?

74. The author journaled: "All the technology in the world will not substitute for thinking, caring people who are done letting their planet be destroyed." What do you think?

75. The author wrote: "Live your life empowered in every dimension." What do you suppose the empowerment dimensions of your life may be?

76. Discuss what you think the author meant by the words and book title, *Empowered: One Planet at a Time*. What do these words mean to you?

AFTERWORD

77. The authors of the Afterword wrote: "…we were positive about finding a way *together* rather than expecting things *not* to work because it was too difficult to cross language, political, or cultural barriers." Can you think of examples in the world today where these words have been put into action? How might this perspective help you move forward on an issue that matters to you?

78. Discuss the idea shared by the authors of the Afterword in which the world seems to both expand and shrink as a result of their collaboration. Do you think collaborating among people in the same country would result in something similar?

79. Describe how you feel about the following sentences: "We ask you to keep in mind there are millions—even billions—of people who simply do not have the time to care about their environment because they are struggling to live and care for their children. If you are reading this book, then you have a chance to apply yourself in ways others may never be able to locally or across our planet."

WRAP UP

80. Consider the artwork on each of the six chapter cover pages. Discuss how you believe each art panel represents their respective chapter theme. Then, consider the complete poster shown on the page, "About the Art and Artist." View it in color at the referenced website for full impact. Describe your reaction when you discovered that each of the six panels combine to create one single artistic work. Discuss symbolism found in the complete artistic

work. How do you believe this art relates to the core messages of *Empowered: One Planet at a Time*?

81. Reflect on your discussion of question #1 above related to Aberdeen Leary's theme, "We Cannot Be Too Loud." What do you think about her message now? How does her theme appear in the artwork in this book?

82. What steps will you pledge to take today to begin to put the concepts of this book into action? What difference will it make if you begin today?

83. Would you recommend this book to others? Why or why not? If you believe this book may be helpful to others and/or the causes you care about, what actions will you take to make necessary connections?

ACKNOWLEDGEMENTS

Our family motto inspired me as I wrote this book. We spell out our strength when we need to bolster our courage. We say we are *S-T-R-O-N-G* when we need to remind ourselves and each other that "we are in it together" and "we've got this."

I want to thank numerous people who have helped me on my journey of realizing my dream of writing this book so others may be S-T-R-O-N-G for our planet and future:

Karen Moss, Lynn Johnson, Candace Dreier—for visioning, editing and frequent soul sister support.

Dan Sivek—for helping me bring my vision full circle in a most extraordinary and beautiful way.

Kathleen Dreier—for photographing Dan Sivek's artwork in his studio, preparing the images for publication and, along with my other Dreier Sisters, inspiring me to fly to new heights.

Dieter Böhn, Charly Vogel, and Bernd Schmitt—for steadfast support over these past three decades. Our international friendships have been among the greatest treasures of my life.

Aberdeen Leary—for sharing extraordinary talents and perspective and helping to call the world to action for a brighter future.

Khurram Khan—for knocking my socks off with an amazing cover design.

Jo Seiser—for out-of-the-gate feedback on this book's content and hearty food for thought. You gave me tremendous momentum.

Sharon Schwab and Susan Wurzer—for helping me see new horizons and lifting my dreams higher.

Karin Sieg—for wind beneath my wings on this journey as my longest (not oldest) friend.

Linda Barnes—for sharing your deep love of Earth, our timeless friendship, and your willingness to review this book for college classroom use.

Jennifer Brilowski—for your willingness to share this book with your daughter to enhance her home school experience and help her rise as a young leader.

Spencer Johnson—for tutoring me on graphic art and propelling me toward the finish line.

Emma Dreier, Jake Werner, John Moss, Eleanor Knippel, Kami McCarthy, Abbey Leary, and Amber Dreier—for being my team of insightful young adults who evaluated this book's draft content and cover design. You were my guides. Continue to show us the way....

Last, but certainly not least, I thank Tom Dreier—for helping me fulfill a promise we made around a campfire in 1981.

REFERENCES

These resources have contributed to the author's development of the concepts and practices shared through *Empowered: One Planet at a Time.* The author is grateful for the works and research of others before her. They have given her shoulders to stand on.

Boyd, D. R. (2015). *The optimistic environmentalist: Progressing towards a greener future.* Toronto, ON: ECW Press.

Brower, D., & Chapple, S. (1995). *Let the mountains talk, let the rivers run: A call to those who would save the earth.* New York, NY: Harper Collins West.

Brower, D. R., Collins, L., & Schweitzer, M. (1975). *Only a little planet.* New York, NY: Ballantine Books, a division of Random House, Inc.

Burchard, B. (2017). *High performance habits.* Carlsbad, CA: Hay House, Inc.

Country Beautiful (Eds.). (1975). *Great wilderness days in the words of John Burroughs.* Waukesha, WI: Country Beautiful.

Jackson, M. (2015). *While the glaciers slept: Being human in a time of climate change.* Brattleboro, VT: Green Writers Press.

Kanze, E. (1996). *The world of John Burroughs: The life and work of one of America's greatest naturalists.* New York, NY: Sierra Club Books & Random House, Inc.

Kaplan, R., & Kaplan, S. (1989). *The experience of nature: A psychological perspective.* Cambridge, NY: Cambridge University Press.

Klein, N. (2014). *This changes everything: Capitalism vs the climate.* New York, NY: Simon & Schuster Paperbacks.

Lewis, C. A. (1996). *Green nature human nature.* Urbana and Chicago, IL: University of Illinois Press.

Loeb, P. R. (2010). *Soul of a citizen: Living with conviction in challenging times.* New York, NY: St. Martin's Griffin.

Machlis, G. E., & Jarvis, J. B. (2018). *The future of conservation in America: A chart for rough waters.* Chicago, IL: The University of Chicago Press.

Maxwell, J. C. (2015). *Intentional living: Choosing a life that matters.* New York, NY: Center Street, Hachette Book Group.

Maxwell, J. C. (2017). *The power of significance: How purpose changes your life.* New York, NY: Center Street.

Maxwell, J. C., & Dornan, J. (1997). *Becoming a person of influence: How to positively impact the lives of others.* New York, NY: HarperCollins Leadership.

McKibben, B. (2011). *Eaarth.* New York, NY: St. Martin's Press.

Nelson, G., Senator. (1970). *America's last chance.* Waukesha, WI: Country Beautiful.

Northwest Earth Institute. (2008). *Discussion course in voluntary simplicity.* Portland, OR: Northwest Earth Institute.

Rome, A. (2013). *The genius of Earth Day: How a 1970 teach-in unexpectedly made the first green generation.* New York, NY: Hill and Wang.

Roszak, T. (2001). *The voice of the earth: An exploration of ecopsychology.* Grand Rapids, MI: Phanes Press, Inc.

Roszak, T., Gomes, M. E., & Kanner, A. D. (Eds.). (1995). *Ecopsychology: Restoring the earth, healing the mind.* San Francisco, CA: Sierra Club Books.

Savory, A. (2013, March 4). How to green the world's deserts and reverse climate change. [YouTube video]. *TED Talk.* Retrieved January 16, 2019, from https://www.youtube.com/watch?v=vpTHi7O66pI

Wilson, E. O. (1984). *Biophilia.* Cambridge, MA: Harvard University Press.

Wilson, E. O. (2002). *The future of life.* New York, NY: Alfred A. Knopf

ABOUT THE ART AND ARTIST—
BY DAN SIVEK

"Empowered" is painted in pastel - highly concentrated, durable, and permanent pigment held together with a binder. In this painting, I used more than thirty different colors of pastels. My greatest challenge in painting "Empowered" was to create a painting that could be separated into six parts to symbolize the book's six chapters. I began by creating a sketch based on reading the book and on Patty's suggestions. Then came another sketch and another. With each sketch, transitions became smoother and the symbolism clearer. One surprise occurred as I painted the hill to the left of the mountains. Originally, it was simply a hill, but as it took shape, I recognized it as the shape of Mount Kilimanjaro, a welcome African connection.

I've immersed myself in nature since childhood. Throughout school, but mostly in high school, I cultivated my natural skills in art. Most of my career has been as an environmental educator teaching learners the knowledge and skills needed to solve environmental issues. I've worked in camps, nature centers, a state natural resource agency, and at a state university. During this time, I sketched and sculpted in wood. Later, I switched paths and pursued art full time, often immersing myself in nature to inspire my artistic works in pencil, pastel, watercolor, acrylic, oil and wood. I live in a partially solar-heated home surrounded by native prairie and woodland I see every day through my studio window. I encourage you to follow your heart and be moved by Patty's words to do all you can for Earth and all her inhabitants.

See the "Empowered" painting at www.bluespring.life.

ABOUT THE AUTHOR

Patty Dreier deeply cares about people and our Earth which is why she dedicated her life's capstone to empowering people to stand up for their planet and themselves. She believes that for young people to have a brighter future, they must be equipped and supported as change makers who will bravely and confidently step up to help us face challenges and seize opportunities. This is why she wrote *Empowered: One Planet at a Time* for young adults and their teachers and mentors.

Over the past thirty years as an educator and leader, including eight years as an elected official representing 71,000 citizens in central Wisconsin, Patty has helped thousands of people of all ages build their knowledge and skills to stand up on local and global issues that matter to them. Sharing her local, state, national, and international experiences, she inspires readers to see themselves as citizens of Planet Earth with all the authority they need to be powerful agents for change. She has a Master of Science degree in Natural Resource Management/Environmental Education from the University of Wisconsin-Stevens Point and is certified by John C. Maxwell as a coach, teacher, and speaker. The whole Earth is her home. Connect with Patty at www.bluespring.life.

EMPOWERED: ONE PLANET

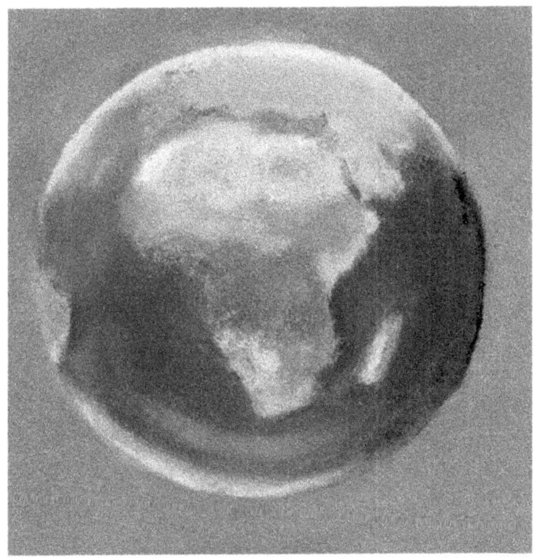

"The planet you're standing on
looking out at the stars
is the earth...

hanging in nothing
the way a bubble hangs
in the air."

--Lawrence Collins from *Only a little planet*, 1975,
Ballantine Books

STAND UP.
CREATE A MOVEMENT.
ONE PLANET AT A TIME.
WWW.BLUESPRING.LIFE

- Take the Free Courage and Confidence Assessment.

- Download Checklists for Individual and Team Action Projects.

- Get Your Free E-Journal.

- Get Resources for Teachers and Mentors.

- Help Move the *Empowered: One Planet at a Time* Movement: Lead and Participate in Workshops, On-Line Courses and Certificate Programs.

- Inspire Others with Your Story.

- And More!

CPSIA information can be obtained
at www.ICGtesting.com
Printed in the USA
LVHW042127130123
737045LV00002B/262